Abundant, Exalted, Immeasurable

Pasanno Bhikkhu

Abhayagiri Buddhist Monastery
16201 Tomki Road
Redwood Valley, California 95470
www.abhayagiri.org
707-485-1630

© 2016 Abhayagiri Buddhist Monastery

First Edition, printed in Malaysia 2017

Page 199 constitutes a continuation of the copyright page.

ISBN 978-1-63271-011-6
ISBN 978-1-63271-012-3 (eBook)

Cover by Sumi Shin.

sabbadānaṃ dhammadānaṃ jināti
The gift of Dhamma excels all gifts

Dedicated with immeasurable gratitude to all mothers:
past, present and to come.

Contents

Abbreviations

Foreword

Even as a mother protects with her life
her child, her only child . . .

That boundless, unconditional love of a mother: an image that I will forever carry in my heart is of my own mother as she waited for death to relieve her of a tired and malfunctioning body. Only four days before her passing, she sat on the edge of the bed in the evening in an attempt to find a moment of comfort or ease after a long day. As I sat next to her, the tears I had been hoping to hold spilled forth. I blurted out the sense of impending loss I was feeling, how much I would miss her. In that instant her own discomfort and suffering were forgotten. Some hidden energy source lifted her body from its slight slouch. She put her arm around me to comfort me and reminded me: "We carry each other in our hearts."

When Luang Por Pasanno completed the teaching of the retreat that is the source of this book in September of 2008, a handful of us declared enthusiastically that we would produce a book so others could also benefit from this retreat. Time passed. My mother passed. The idea to put these teachings into a book resurfaced, but this time with a deeper intention. It felt like a wonderful tribute to my mother, to all mothers—whether from a biological mother or someone who has fit the ideal, perhaps a father, aunt, uncle, older sibling, friend, or teacher—as an expression of the gratitude for the example and the love.

Many have contributed generously to the development of the book: the transcribers, various editors, layout team, and proofreaders—in particular, I'd like to thank Tom Lane for his monumental effort in editing, Hisayo Suzuki for her sharp eye and mind with the line editing, and Sumi Shin for the creative and expressive cover design. I am grateful to all who participated and contributed in this wonderful community effort. This offering is in honor of mothers, past, present, and to come. It represents a beautiful transference of the energy of love and gratitude into something produced for the benefit of others, seen and unseen.

We are all very grateful for the limitless generosity that Luang Por exemplifies when teaching the Dhamma.

Refuges and Precepts

The refuges of Buddha, Dhamma, and Sangha
provide the foundation for the wholesome
qualities of the heart to arise.

I'd like to welcome everyone who has gathered for this occasion and to express appreciation to Susan, Karen, and Cassidy for pulling it together and prodding me into giving a retreat. This is the second retreat I've led in California in twelve years. The theme is *mettā*, loving-kindness, and the context is a retreat, a practice situation. We are taking the opportunity to explore the different expressions, development, and implications of loving-kindness.

As I understand it, we can't extract loving-kindness out of the Buddha's teachings as an orphan that stands alone. It doesn't work that way. We pick up a corner of the Buddha's teachings and everything comes along with it, including mettā. It's like I pick up this little tassel here and, of course, everything connected to it starts coming up as well—everything's attached. Pretty soon, the cushion, the bell, everything comes along with it.

The teachings of loving-kindness are within a whole context and setting. Of course, one of the most important foundations for any aspect of the teaching to arise out of is what we've just done: determining the refuges and precepts. It's not just a curious little ceremony that we begin a retreat with and that's the end of it. The refuges of Buddha, Dhamma, and Sangha provide the foundation for the wholesome qualities of the heart to arise. The precepts establish a strong foundation of integrity and virtue, as well as an ability to cultivate, both individually and in a group setting, a sense of trust: trust in oneself and the whole environment that one is in.

Reflecting on and recollecting the Buddha, Dhamma, and Sangha as refuges is always an important reminder for us. The reality is that we are always taking refuge in something, whether it is in some distraction or particular worry or fear. The mind goes there, and that's where we create our refuge. We rely on it and build our lives around it.

As we find out, that's not a very satisfying refuge, but it's what we do as human beings. It's like Ajahn Chah's definition of what a human being is: "A human being is a being with issues." It's always having an issue with something or other. It keeps us busy and gives us something to live for. And then we die—it goes on and on.

So, we redirect our attention to something that is a worthy refuge: the Buddha as a historical figure and symbol of fundamental qualities, such as wisdom, compassion, and purity. The first line of one of the morning chants we do at the monastery is *Buddho, susuddho karuṇāmahaṇṇavo. Buddho* is one who knows, one with wisdom. *Susuddho* is purity, and *karuṇāmahaṇṇavo*, great compassion.

Even the recitation *namo tassa bhagavato arahato sammāsambuddhassa* refers to those qualities. *Bhagavato* is the Blessed One, who radiates the blessing and heart quality of compassion. *Arahato* is one who is far from defiling tendencies and thus, pure. *Sammāsambuddhassa* refers to the self-enlightened, wisdom quality.

The traditional recollections of the Buddha always refer to these qualities of wisdom, compassion, and purity. Of course, these are not qualities belonging solely to the Buddha, but the Buddha is the archetype of what is most fruitful for us to cultivate, pay attention to, and use to create a balance within the heart.

Wisdom, compassion, and purity are the qualities that we cultivate and pay attention to if we reflect on how our practice is doing and how our life is going. Are these qualities being attended to? Am I out of balance or missing something? If so, how can I reconfigure that, so I pay attention to those aspects of the Buddha?

The Dhamma is the teaching in a conventional sense and also the underlying truth of existence. There are fundamental truths that we are able to realize, understand, and penetrate, and when those truths are seen and understood, they have a transformative quality to them. The Buddha himself said that whether a Buddha arises in the world or not, there is still this underlying nature of things. All compounded things are impermanent and unsatisfactory. All *dhammas*, all things, are not-self.

It's helpful when a Buddha comes along and points it out, but this is also the underlying truth, the way things are. We can direct our attention to and realize these fundamental truths.

The Sangha as a refuge, on a conventional level, consists of ordained people who have stepped out of the world and made a commitment to spiritual practice and training. Having these examples is a helpful tool. This is a monastic retreat in the sense of having the monastic sangha here. We have our own particular perspectives. Some people find it useful, but it's not everybody's cup of tea. This is an opportunity to get a bit of the flavor of having ordained sangha nearby.

However, when the Buddha refers to sangha outside of the conventional level, he's again pointing to qualities of the heart. In our morning chant, when we recollect Sangha, we say: *Supaṭipanno bhagavato sāvakasaṅgho*, the Sangha of the Blessed One's disciples are those who practice well; *ujupaṭipanno*, practice directly; *ñāyapaṭipanno*, practice for the overcoming of suffering, for understanding and knowledge; *sāmīcipaṭipanno*, practice appropriately, with integrity. These are also the qualities of those who have entered into the fruition of the path: stream-enterers, once-returners, nonreturners, and arahants.

When we come together to practice in a retreat situation, we take on the eight precepts for the duration of the retreat. There's a simplification that takes place, having the eight precepts as a foundation. There's a very interesting discourse that the Buddha gave to Visākhā, one of his foremost female disciples. He was praising the lay community's keeping of the lunar observance days once a week. In Pali, it's called the *Uposatha*. Traditionally, laypeople would take the eight precepts in the morning and keep them for a day and a night.

The way the Buddha described it is that the arahants, who are fully enlightened, live their whole lives not harming, not taking the life of any living creature. Laypeople are able to live just like arahants for a day and a night, not taking the life of any living creature. Arahants live their whole lives not taking what isn't given, not stealing, and committed to honesty. For a day and a night, you are able to live just like an enlightened being, refraining from taking that which is not given—and so on, through all the eight precepts.

This is basically how enlightened beings live; it's their hard-wired structure. For us to gather for a week of practicing together is a very special opportunity. Sometimes there is not much reflection when we ask someone how a retreat went. They'll say, "Oh, my mind was all over the place; there was this ache and pain; there was this, and there was that." Nobody says, "Well, I lived for a week in simplicity, living like the noble ones. It was great." It ends up being hopelessly enmeshed in "me" and "my mind."

It's no small thing to be able to say, "I got this opportunity to live simply for this week. It was great." It has a wonderful effect. We are also doing it in an ideal, heavenly world here, surrounded by a lovely forest.

We have this opportunity to come and practice walking and sitting meditation together, having taken on the refuges and precepts. The theme is loving-kindness, and I would encourage everybody to approach this whole time of practice together within this sphere of loving-kindness. Use walking and sitting meditation to bring up the quality of kindness.

Traditionally, in the classical modes of cultivating loving-kindness, the first person you generate loving-kindness towards is yourself. So just be kind to yourself during this period of retreat. It's a great opportunity to have time for solitude and quiet like this, to cultivate mindfulness and continuity of awareness. Enjoy it. Don't tie yourself up in knots.

I think loving-kindness can't be separated from the Dhamma or anything else. Those qualities of letting go, non-contention: that's where loving-kindness arises. When we let go of our moods, obsessions, worries, and fears—what's left? Loving-kindness. We aren't contending, struggling, and fighting—feeling in opposition to the weather, the circumstances, the people we are with, or ourselves, internally. There's just that non-contention, that non-struggle, that non-irritation. The quality of loving-kindness is able to arise quite naturally as a result.

It's a good idea to review how we're holding the meditation as we begin the practice. As we take time to establish and recollect the context of sitting here, just relaxing the body and awareness, ask, "Where am I holding, where am I tightening?" Say, "Okay, let's just relax and settle." Take a couple of minutes sweeping through the body, paying attention: "Let's just relax here, let's get settled." Breath coming in and going out; tune in to the breath and allow that feeling of settling to establish itself. Then establish continuity of awareness with the object of meditation.

I imagine that everybody here has experience in meditation. People will have their own particular methods they are comfortable or familiar with. My own inclination and ease of familiarity are with mindfulness of breathing, so if I am giving instruction, I will almost invariably use that as a framework in formal meditation.

If you are using a different object for some reason, it's easy to extrapolate the instruction for mindfulness of breathing and turn it to whatever method or technique that you are using. It's very similar with walking meditation. Find a comfortable spot. If you like being in the shade, be in the shade. If you like being in the sun, be in the sun. Find a path that's nice and level and long enough that you feel comfortable—twenty, twenty-five, thirty paces, or whatever. If it's too long, it's easy for the mind to start wandering. If it's too short, it's difficult to get settled, going back and forth all the time. Find something that's comfortable for you.

The underlying theme is how to make it comfortable, bringing ease into the practice, whether it's walking or sitting. Or, if you like standing meditation, you can do standing meditation. Again, it's not so much the posture or the method: it's how you approach establishing the mind, bringing attention to the object of meditation, sustaining and working with continuity. Where does the mind go? Does it drift? Does it get loose and nebulous? Or does it home in on the minutiae of the mind and get tied up and tight?

Pay attention to what the mind is doing. Balance is an important quality to bring to the practice. How can you best sustain that continuity of awareness? That's where the mind becomes peaceful. It doesn't become peaceful just by forcing the mind onto an object and holding it there. Even if you succeed in doing that, it doesn't actually make the mind that peaceful.

For the mind to settle, there needs to be a balance of interested application of energy and ease. If there's too much forcing, it creates tension; if it's too loose, the mind gets nebulous and cloudy and drifts. We need to balance the mind by working with what is.

Whether it's sitting, walking, standing, or lying down, continuity starts to kick in and allows the mind to settle. The Buddha talks about cultivation of mindfulness in all four postures. It's essential to develop continuity in the different postures.

I remember the first year I was a monk: the evening meeting at the monastery where I was would be an hour sitting, an hour standing, and an hour walking, with some chanting at the beginning or end. That would be the evening meeting—an hour each. I remember when I first started, I thought, "Wow, great. They do standing meditation. Man, that's going to be good. My knees kill me when I'm sitting."

Then I realized that the pain just goes somewhere else. What bodies do is get uncomfortable. What is needed is to relax around the pain or the discomfort and cultivate kindness.

There was one Rains Retreat I did when I had about fifteen or twenty years as a monk, during which I did several months of lying-down meditation. I had fractured my pelvis, so I wasn't doing anything else. But I was in very quiet, peaceful surroundings. I had lobbied the doctor, who was a supporter of the monastery, and he had sprung me out of the hospital and got me back to the monastery. I had said, "Whether I'm in the hospital or at the monastery, I'm going to be lying down anyway. I'll be a lot happier out at the monastery."

We realize that what's important is the continuity of the awareness and the quality of the attention that we pay to things. It's not getting a particular posture or technique down. The techniques and postures are essential, but they're tools, and it's how you use a tool that's important. During the week that we have here, pay attention. "How am I holding the meditation? How am I holding the perception? How am I holding my body? How am I holding the things that are coming up in my own mind? How am I holding the perceptions that I have of the people around me?" That's what is really important.

The mind in a mettā retreat can think, "All those other people are peaceful. How come I'm not peaceful?" Of course, everybody else is thinking the same thing: "All these other people look like they're happy and kind; they're really getting loving-kindness. I'm obviously not getting it."

We can take loving-kindness as a theme, and then sometimes, what comes up is how irritating the world is. But it doesn't really matter. How are we holding it? What is actually coming up in the mind, and how are we relating to it? How are we layering our experience? That's where the kindness is, having that sense of non-contention, letting go: "This is what's coming up? Oh, that can be let go of. I don't have to contend with that. Back to the breath, back to the walking, back to the continuity of awareness."

These are a few reflections to begin the retreat with.

Mettā: A Mature Emotion

Question: My activist neighbor is going to Nevada to register voters. It's difficult to convince myself that I'm sitting in meditation for the benefit of all beings (not just giving myself a "gift"), let alone explain a week of sitting to her. Could you comment?

Answer: There are a couple of different layers there. The main one that leaps out is that I don't think you need to explain yourself to everybody, especially in the light of loving-kindness. It is usually not an act of loving-kindness to try to compare and then explain yourself to others. That's usually an exercise in judgment of yourself in which you, invariably, come up short. The very impulse to have to explain yourself to others is almost always generated from the sense, "I must be doing something wrong, and therefore, I have to explain myself." You're inevitably going to come up short.

A good question is: "Is this an act of kindness towards myself?" And then, "Is it a real act of kindness to explain myself to other people? Do they actually need to know?" It's something of an American compulsion to explain yourself to others.

I remember the very first year that I came to America to help found Abhayagiri. We were invited on almsround to a neighbor's house, which is about seven miles from the monastery. You walk down Tomki Road and East Road on almsround to get to their house. It's a long walk. A woman pulled over and asked, "Where are you going? Do you need a ride?" I had misjudged the time and we were running a bit late, so it was quite good to have a ride. There was still maybe a mile or a mile and a half left. It wasn't that far, but in the distance of a mile or a mile and a half, I learned more about that woman's life than I had wanted to know. I had never seen her before. There is a compulsion in the American psyche to try to explain everything to everybody. I don't know how much of a kindness that is to other people.

So these are some basic thoughts in terms of the reflection around loving-kindness: "Is it a kindness to oneself? Is it a kindness to others?"

In the realm of meditation and activism, we can ask ourselves: "What is better? What should I be doing?" There's a tendency in the mind to think in terms of either/or. Either I should be doing this, or I should be doing that. Either this is right and that's wrong or that's wrong and this is right.

That approach is very divisive and complicates things. Again, is it a kindness to think in that way? It's a real questioning of the underlying ways that we relate to ourselves and the world around us: what is the effect of that framework of right and wrong, either/or? It's important in terms of spiritual practice, particularly from this perspective of loving-kindness, to get some space around that way of dividing things up—separating them out and being in opposition to things.

I don't think that is a helpful way to reflect on our experience because how the Buddha structured things was not so much as right and wrong, but more as skillful and unskillful, wholesome and unwholesome. We realize that an activist who is registering voters is doing something wholesome and skillful. That's a good thing to do.

"Is it what I need to be doing? Is it what I want to be doing right now? Do I feel drawn to that?" Maybe yes, maybe no. It's also about being able to see somebody else's skillfulness or wholesome activity and delight in that, being able to derive a sense of encouragement from others' good actions without intimidating ourselves: "Other people can and are happy to do that. That's great. What I'd like to do for this week, at least, is to have a chance for a period of retreat—settling, creating an inner anchor for myself. That's a wholesome, good, and skillful thing to do." It doesn't mean that because we have made the choice to be on retreat that we're right and the rest of those schmucks out there really blew it. These are very separate realms.

We can encourage ourselves in the choices that we make without undermining ourselves. That's an act of kindness. We can also see how other people choose to use their time and energy and encourage and support them, or at least delight in the good that they are doing. That is an aspect of our own wholesomeness as well, and we benefit from that.

There is a word in Buddhist jargon: in Pali, it is *puñña*, in the Thai language, *boon*. Inevitably, Thai people who have been to the West or have met a Westerner who is studying Buddhism ask, "How do you translate *boon*?" It's one of those very difficult terms to render. But the Buddha himself said, "*Puñña* is another word for happiness." (A 7.62) It is the result of skillful action: good, wholesome actions or activities that result in happiness and well-being for you and for others.

Generosity and giving are puñña. Keeping precepts and virtue are puñña. Meditation is puñña. Listening to teachings is puñña. Teaching is puñña. Giving the opportunity for other people to access teachings is puñña. Helping others, acts of service, are puñña. Delighting in the good that other people do is puñña. Dedicating the blessings that come from your own good actions is puñña.

There are many levels, but these are avenues for creating happiness. We realize that we can tie them into the theme of loving-kindness. The recognition of that which is wholesome and skillful is an act of loving-kindness, as well as the commitment to doing those acts—also realizing that the thought, "If I'm not meditating, I'm wasting my time," is not a fixed thing.

There are many avenues of wholesome and skillful action, and it's important to be able to have a recognition of the spectrum, so that we can seize the opportunities, such as seeing somebody else doing something skillful and then delighting in that. It's expressed in the Pali word *anumodana*, delighting in the good that is done. You don't even have to do anything.

If you see somebody else doing something skillful, it doesn't have to be intimidating: "I just don't measure up." Nor do you have to be jealous: "They're not so good, really." There is that sort of criticism, which is a way to pull people down and put them in their place. It's very small-minded; it's not kind to yourself and not kind to others.

Conversely, there is a spaciousness in the heart when you are neither intimidated by others nor torturing yourself because you are not doing quite the "right" thing in the "right" way. Feeling guilty about something that you didn't do properly just goes on and on. None of that is a kindness to yourself or to others.

I remember one time traveling as a translator and attendant to a very senior, well-known, and highly respected Thai monk, Luang Por Paññānanda. A few people in the room here have met him before. When I took a group to Thailand, we went to pay respects to him. Now, there is someone with serious puñña, a whole life of giving. When we went, he was sick and in the hospital, but it was a hospital that he had built. He was about ninety-six at the time, but very bright.

I traveled with him in the 1980s and one time we were in New Zealand. It was the evening session: chanting, meditation, Dhamma talk, and questions afterwards. One of the questions that somebody asked fairly early on was: "How do we deal with that feeling of guilt?" Of course, I was familiar with that feeling, but the interesting thing was that when I tried to translate it, I realized that I didn't know what the word for guilt is in Thai. I had been translating for teachers and studying the language and the Dhamma for years, but my mind drew a blank, so I burst out laughing. I explained to him what the question was, why I was laughing, and how the concept was a bit distant in the Thai language and culture. I had to explain to him what Westerners do with their minds to make themselves feel guilty.

He listened and got this very concerned look on his face as I was explaining how guilt works. When I finished the explanation, he said, "Oh, that's really suffering. Tell them not to do that." It isn't as if Thai people don't have these emotions. There is a very healthy place for remorse, but not that complication of guilt, which is so easy to carry around because of the strong sense of self, "me," and judgment. We judge, compare, and divide ourselves into "me" and this world that we are either trying to live up to or being intimidated by. These are very painful distinctions.

An act of loving-kindness comes with the attitude of "this is the way things are," in the sense that there is a recognition: "Well, that's just a feeling. I'm going to get some space around that, not contend with it, and not slip into those thoughts of comparison and suffering that accompany it." That is an act of loving-kindness towards oneself. It's a very useful skill to be able to see somebody who is doing something good and then be able not to make it a judgment about yourself, torturing yourself.

I think that sometimes, when we see loving-kindness as one of the *brahmavihāras*, the divine abidings, that puts it out *there* somewhere: "The divine, that's way off somewhere else." One of the monks in England has started translating brahmavihāra as "mature emotion," and that's a skillful way of bringing attention to that aspect. It is a mature emotion to be able to turn attention to loving-kindness, compassion, sympathetic joy, and equanimity. The doorway into them all is the quality of loving-kindness. Bring attention to that, consciously, and then also bring attention to what obstructs it. We can start to pay attention to the immature emotions, which are fairly accessible, and recognize: "There's that twinge of jealousy; there's that twinge of comparing; there's that irritation." Rather than letting them gain momentum, you can ask: "How can I bring a mature emotion into this? How can I create some space around this?"

The quality of loving-kindness creates space; it's a very spacious emotion. As we create that spaciousness, it's also very solid. It's not a fleeting kind of pleasure, delight, or gratification. Irritation, jealousy, and aversion come up in the mind, but they don't create a steadiness. They're not stable feelings and emotions in the heart.

With that feeling of loving-kindness—as we tap into and direct attention to it—we realize there is a stability and groundedness that comes from it. We have a ground beneath that is not shaken by the vagaries of either the internal world of our emotions and reactions or the external world of change and praise and blame. When I think of people I've met who embodied loving-kindness, there was a tremendous steadiness or stability there.

Thinking of something being billed as a "Mettā Retreat," what do we do? Do we come and ooze niceness? That turns my stomach, actually. Or do we put a lot of effort into trying to beam love everywhere? That can get pretty tiring. Again, the people I've met who embodied loving-kindness possessed tremendous stability.

I think of one particular circumstance in my life that was very helpful and illuminating for me. I had been the abbot of the International Forest Monastery in Thailand for a few years, not all that long, and I was finding it overwhelming. I had a chance to go to England. Ajahn Sumedho and many of the other senior western monks, old mates, were there. I was still stuck in Thailand looking after a monastery. I wasn't sure whether I was capable of doing it, or if I even wanted to do it. There were conflicts with the monks and duties with the lay community. I was feeling overwhelmed.

Toward the end of my stay in England, which was just a few weeks, I was dreading getting on the plane. It was going to be a miserable plane ride because I was thinking: "Oh, I've got to go back to the monastery, and there's this monk and that monk, and blah, blah, blah." One of the senior monks in England, who had lived in Thailand for many years, had a little package. He said, "When you get to Bangkok, please take this and offer it to this particular monk." This monk, Phra Payutto, had a good reputation, but I hadn't met him yet. He was also not so well known at that time. Now, he is internationally renowned.

In those days he lived in a temple in Bangkok at the edge of Chinatown, in the old central part of the city. The area that he was in wasn't particularly nice. Oftentimes in Bangkok, all of the monks' shops are in one area and then there is another area that is the clothing section. The place where the temple was looked like they fixed the transmissions of car engines there. Oil, grease, and car parts were everywhere as you entered the temple. One of the things the temple also did was cremations for the poorest of the poor people. There was always something happening, and it was crowded.

I went to the back, where his dwelling place was. He radiated peace and kindness in the center of this business, dirtiness, pollution, and chaos. He was an anchor of peace, clarity, and kindness. Talking to him, he was extraordinarily kind, and he received me very well. He's now very well-known and respected in Thailand. People come from all levels of society to pay respects to him. He's one of the very few monks in Thailand to have completed all of his studies of the scriptures and Pali when he was still a novice. When that happens, the King is traditionally the sponsor for the ordination. He has a brilliant mind. Sometimes, somebody with a brilliant mind is not necessarily attuned to other people, but he had a real completeness; everything was suffused with kindness.

It really struck me: "Okay, that's a way that I can survive. If I could turn my attention to those qualities of kindness and mettā, that would hold me in good stead. Also, I'm going back to a quiet forest monastery in the northeast of Thailand, and if I can't get some peace out of that, I'm doing something wrong with my holy life." He was a wonderful example.

Some of the people here also met him when I took the group to Thailand. He received us so graciously. He is in constant pain; he has always been plagued by illness. But although he is in constant pain, the quality of kindness that radiates from him is very tangible.

You see, again, the sense of a mature emotion that is very steadying, stabilizing, and grounding. These are not qualities that people are born with. It's not that they get it all; these are universal qualities that anybody can cultivate and tap into. I think it's an important reflection to develop: "Oh, this is a mature emotion to direct attention to." It gives us the opportunity, whether one is in a family or social situation, whether it's dealing with Buddhists, people in society, or oneself, to be able to direct attention to this very important quality.

Mindfulness Immersed in the Body

*The natural rhythm of the breath suffuses the
body with a sense of warmth and energy.*

I thought I would begin the morning teaching with a reflection
from the Buddha concerning mindfulness of the body.

"Bhikkhus, even as one who encompasses with his mind the great
ocean includes thereby all the streams that run into the ocean, just
so, whoever develops and cultivates mindfulness directed to the
body includes all wholesome qualities that pertain to true knowledge.

"Bhikkhus, one thing, when developed and cultivated, leads to
a strong sense of urgency . . . leads to great good . . . leads to great
security from bondage . . . leads to mindfulness and clear comprehension . . . leads to the attainment of knowledge and vision . . .
leads to a pleasant dwelling in this very life . . . leads to the realization of the fruit of knowledge and liberation. What is that one
thing? Mindfulness directed to the body. This is the one thing that,
when developed and cultivated, leads to the realization of the fruit
of knowledge and liberation.

"Bhikkhus, when one thing is developed and cultivated, the
body becomes tranquil, the mind becomes tranquil, thought and
examination subside, and all wholesome qualities that pertain to
true knowledge reach fulfillment by development. What is that
one thing? Mindfulness directed to the body. When this one thing
is developed and cultivated, the body becomes tranquil . . . and all
wholesome qualities that pertain to true knowledge reach fulfillment by development.

"Bhikkhus, when one thing is developed and cultivated, ignorance is abandoned . . . true knowledge arises . . . the conceit 'I
am' is abandoned . . . the underlying tendencies are uprooted . . .
the fetters are abandoned. What is that one thing? Mindfulness
directed to the body. When this one thing is developed and cultivated, the fetters are abandoned."

(A 1:575, 1:576–582, 1:583, 1:586–590)

These are very useful reflections because although the theme
of this retreat is mettā, loving-kindness, it's essential to have an
anchor, a stable base or foundation to work from. Sometimes, trying
to direct attention to a mental state or an emotion is like trying
to grab the wind—it slips right through your fingers. But having a
good grounding in the quality of mindfulness that is focused on the
body, you have a firm basis to build from. As the Buddha said, all of
these wholesome qualities arise out of that mindfulness directed to
the body. Once you have a stable base, then you have a foundation
for building wholesome mental states.

Even if you are doing mettā as a meditation, you still need to
have an anchor. You still need to be grounded in something and
have someplace to keep returning to, which is mindfulness of the
body. Become very familiar with returning to the body.

There are many ways of using mindfulness of the body, but in
terms of the formal practice of meditation, become familiar with
mindfulness of breathing and bring attention to the breathing process. Sit and pay attention to the breath coming into the body: the
sensation of the breath as it touches the tip of the nose, as it passes
through the nasal passages, the back of the throat, down into the
chest, the abdomen rising. Pay attention to breathing out: the abdomen falling, the sensation in the body, the chest area, throat, tip
of the nose, the breath going out. Tune in to that rhythm of the
breath. Not forcing the breath, not trying to regulate the breath,
just attend to the breath as you are experiencing it.

There is a tendency for us to try to regulate, oversee, or maintain the breath in some way, but that's adding an extra layer of complication. Unless you're dead, you are going to be breathing, so it happens anyway. Just tune in to the breath: allow the sense of relaxing into the breathing. Also recognize that the breathing takes place within the whole sphere of the body. You are sitting here and breathing, but it isn't as if there's just a nose suspended in space somewhere: you have the rest of your body sitting here. How are you holding it? What does it feel like? Is it comfortable? Is it uncomfortable? Does it feel spacious? Does it feel contracted? What does the body feel like? Is there some tension in the face, in the shoulders? Is it relaxed? Can you soften that? What does it feel like in the abdomen?

Relax the abdomen. It's quite interesting; the more comfortable we are with breathing, relaxing, and settling, our posture gets better over time. It feels natural and balanced. You don't need to strain to hold the posture upright and make yourself sit up straight. It's obviously necessary, to some degree, to try to keep an upright posture, but if there is too much force or straining, it gets uncomfortable to sit straight. But as you keep relaxing, softening, and releasing tension, you find that the body naturally lines up quite nicely because that's the most comfortable way to sit for three-quarters of an hour, an hour, or however long one sits in meditation. That's the most natural way for the body to sit.

One of the images helpful in sitting is imagining that there is a string or something similar at the top of your head. If you were dangling from that string, how would the spine and the shoulders line up? It would all be arranged quite neatly, nice and straight. There would be a balance there. The sense of an upright posture is one of comfort and ease as you continue to relax.

The core is the breathing. As you breathe in, allow the breath energy to suffuse the body. The breath comes in, suffusing the body with the feeling of warmth, of energy. As the breath goes out, there is a sense of releasing, relaxing, settling, non-clinging, not holding.

You can't hold on to the breath. You can hold on to it for maybe a minute tops, but you start turning blue, and that's not very comfortable. That natural rhythm of the breath suffuses the body with a sense of warmth and energy. And then, as you breathe out, allow the body to feel suffused with a sense of relaxing, of letting go, releasing.

As we breathe in and we breathe out, the air comes into the body, the air is expelled out of the body. It's released into the atmosphere, whirled around. In the same way, thoughts, impressions, and feelings come into the mind. Allow them to go back out again; release them, let them go. The nature of the breath is to come in and go out. It's the same thing with thoughts, feelings, memories, and perceptions—it's the nature of the mind. We don't have to hold on, cling, or make anything of great importance out of it. We recognize: "That's just a thought, just a memory." It comes into being, and we can let it go out again.

Of course, thoughts and feelings are much stickier than the breath, so it's helpful to have the image of the breath, the feeling of the breath coming in and going out, and then extrapolate that to the feelings, perceptions, memories, and thoughts. They can come in and go out as well.

Then there is a releasing, a spaciousness that is very relaxing, very settling. The mind starts to become clearer, more composed. It's quite natural. When we allow the breath to suffuse the body, allowing the breath to energize and warm it, there is a relaxation that comes into the body. As we allow the mind to have its thoughts and feelings arising and ceasing—coming in and going out—the mind and the heart relax as well.

You don't force the mind to be still or clear. It's through allowing the impressions in the mind to come in and go out without reacting, clinging, or adding a commentary that a natural clarity and spaciousness starts to arise. Allow that to happen. It's an exercise that we need to remind ourselves to do.

Sometimes, when we have meditated for years, it's very easy to get into a rut or a habit. We perceive ourselves in a certain way. We perceive our thoughts and feelings in certain ways, and then we take the bait. I remember Ajahn Chah saying, "Human beings are like fish. A fisherman puts a hook out; it's got a little bit of bait on it, and they go for it every time. Well, actually, they're not like fish at all. When fish take the bait, it only gets caught in their mouth. Humans are more like frogs. Frogs swallow that bait and the hook right down into the gut."

Remember: "I don't need to take the bait." The bait is the feeling of liking and disliking, the feeling of "that's fearful, that's intimidating," "I really like that, I really want that," or "that's important, I can't let that one go." We take the bait.

With that simple process of attending impartially to something as uncomplicated as the breath coming in and the breath going out, you might think, "That's pretty basic. When am I going to get on to the *real* meditation?" But that is what we have to learn how to do: we need to develop the ability to relate to the mind, the world, and the body in a way that we don't get caught in reactions. That is how the mind becomes settled and clear.

That exercise of coming back to the breath, the posture, and the body: how does it feel? Starting from the top of the head, ask: "Is there a sense of tension at the top of the head? The forehead, how can I relax that? What does it feel like around the eyes? Can I relax that? Can I soften that? Around the jaw, around the throat . . ." You are paying attention and recognizing there is breathing—breathing in, breathing out.

What does it feel like in the shoulders, in the arms? What's a comfortable position for the arms? How can I hold them so that they hang comfortably and the hands can be in an easeful position, relaxed and settled?

Feel the breath. Allow the breath to suffuse and soften the body. Allow the chest to be open and spacious, rather than contracting in.

You can see that contraction when you are pondering or recollecting something that has a weight to it, trying to figure it all out. The head comes down and shoulders come in. Bring some space to it, soften, relax. As the breath comes in and the breath goes out, allow it to be open, soft, spacious.

Don't tighten the abdomen. Allow the breath to come down into the abdomen. Allow the breath to affect the whole body, the whole trunk. Breathing in, the abdomen expands, breathing out, it relaxes. If there is tension in the lower back, soften it. Find a balance where holding the posture doesn't take any muscle—you can do this by allowing the trunk of the body to relax and then letting it balance itself on its own.

Oftentimes, people will complain, "My back hurts around the shoulder blades from all this sitting." A lot of that pain is caused by trying to hold the posture using the chest, upper back, or shoulders—trying to *hold* the posture. It gets painful. So relax and allow the spine to rise up out of the pelvis. That is what we have those bones for. They're much easier to look after than the muscles. Let the muscles do what they're going to do and just relax them.

We have all the props: cushions, zafus, and whatever else we need to get a balanced sense of posture and allow the muscles to relax. We can relax into the posture, and then the breathing becomes much more natural. Allow the rhythm to be very natural, not forcing it. Then simply pay attention. Is this a long breath? Is this a short breath? Is it comfortable? Is it uncomfortable?

You don't have to go into any more of an analysis than that. Attend to that: that's soft, that's a bit hard, that's short, that's long. Just familiarize yourself with the breath: that's the in-breath, that's the out-breath. Attend to that, mindfully aware of where you are in the present moment with the breathing process, mindfully aware of the general feeling of the body, again, without going into an analysis and a commentary. This is what it feels like. Does it need to be adjusted? Does it need to be adapted in any way so that it can be a bit more comfortable?

That is enough—sustaining the attention on the breath, the in-breath and the out-breath. It's okay to adjust the posture a bit if necessary, balancing so that you're feeling comfortable. It's important not to strain or to strive too hard because the mind will only truly settle once there's relaxation. You can't bludgeon your mind into submission; it's not going to work. You need to allow it to settle and then attend very mindfully, sustaining the quality of awareness.

It's the quality and continuity of awareness that allows the mind to settle and become peaceful. It's not imposing a concept, your idea of peacefulness, on the mind—that's not going to work.

Instead, relax and learn how to pay attention. Experience the whole body. The breath is what we attend to in a focused way, but in general, there is also the sense of what the whole body is feeling like. Is it nice and straight? Is it balanced? What are the different feelings that come up?

Experience those feelings in the body. Where in the body do we experience anxiety and worry? Where do we feel it? What does it make the body feel like? When a particular desire comes up, where do we feel that? The experience of ill will and aversion in the body: where do we sense that? What does it feel like? The body is a very clear measure of our mental states. If we become more and more attentive, we realize that the different mental states and moods we have are experienced in the body and that we can relax around that.

As you familiarize yourself, you understand: "When my body is tensing like this, when my abdomen gets tight, that's anxiety, that's fear" or "That's worry, that feeling in the chest." The movement towards getting or consuming something creates agitation in the body. In truth, we're not very discerning; we're quite okay with whatever the flavor of the moment is.

However, we can see a repeated pattern of how desire keeps playing itself out by the way that the body is experienced. We can recognize how it works. Tune in to and understand: "There's that feeling in the body." It gives us a clue. Usually when there's a particular fear or desire or aversion, the mind is so quick that it goes right into a story. It has its justifications: "I wouldn't think that if it wasn't *right*." Of course, we have all gotten ourselves into trouble with those kinds of attitudes, and we believe it over and over again.

So tune in to how it is felt in the body. You can experience it without the story, and that is where you can clarify it or allow it to pass through. Again, with the breath, say, "I recognize that feeling." The mind is going to be whispering—probably screaming—its story, but keep coming back to the body and then relaxing, attending, letting it go.

It's very, very simple but very freeing. It's liberating not to be trapped in the stories. The feelings and stories start to cascade. Simplify, coming back to the bodily sensation, the feeling in the body. The breath is that anchor. The in-breath: soothing, nurturing, warming, energizing. The out-breath: releasing, relaxing, expanding. We can tap into that feeling and allow the moods and impressions to dissipate, grounded in awareness in the present moment.

Sometimes we have to deal with physical pain and mental distress. Those are very real experiences. But we still have the breath, which is always neutral. The breath is a neutral base to return to. Can we relax around the physical pain we're experiencing? Are we exacerbating it? Maybe there's illness. Can we actually do anything about it?

Within that sphere of awareness and the neutral quality of the breath, we can be present with that pain. Then, if something needs to be done, we can do it. If not, then we can establish the attitude of not complicating the pain. Sometimes the physical pain can be quite bearable, more so than the mental pain of: "I don't like it. I don't want to be here. It shouldn't be this way. Why me?" We spin ourselves out like that and that's where a lot of pain really is. The actual physical pain is then much more bearable.

Separate these different experiences out. This separation isn't just an intellectual analysis. On an experiential level, by having the anchor of the breath coming in and going out, being grounded, relaxed, and settled in the body, we are able to use discernment. The word that is usually translated as "wisdom" in Buddhism, *paññā*, is probably translated better as "discernment." Use that ability to discern and ask: What's useful and what's not useful right now? What is going to lead to peace? What is going to lead to agitation? We need to be able to discern. Looking and seeing, we are able to recognize that yes, this is the course of action to follow.

Mindfulness of breathing and of the body are anchors for our practice and for the cultivation of loving-kindness. The ability to be present with one in-breath and one out-breath is a tremendous kindness to oneself. The ability to be with the body, to be non-reactive, non-judgmental: that's an act of kindness in the present moment. Being very attentive lays the foundations for the quality of loving-kindness that plays itself out and is manifested in our actions.

There is a very lovely discourse, *Lion's Roar* (A 9:11), where Sāriputta goes to pay respects to the Buddha. He asks to take leave to go wandering on a journey, and the Buddha gives his permission. He goes to prepare himself to leave. Then another monk, who has a grudge against Sāriputta, goes to the Buddha. He says, "Sāriputta hit me and left the monastery." The Buddha sends word to one of the other monks asking him to bring Sāriputta, as there is an accusation against him. The way the Buddha dealt with such issues is interesting in itself. He didn't just dismiss the monk saying, "Sāriputta wouldn't do that."

Sāriputta is brought back. The Buddha explains the accusation. Sāriputta's reply is very moving. He says, "Having developed mindfulness of the body for so long, it is impossible to engage in unskillful action. The mind is well established in loving-kindness, abundant, exalted, measureless, without enmity and ill will."

Sāriputta then gives all sorts of illustrations of the different ways that he has contemplated and developed mindfulness of the body, with the effect that the mind is always in a place of awareness and well-wishing, of compassion towards all beings, making it impossible to have harmed anybody. Sāriputta was extraordinarily skilled in giving illustrations and teachings. Finally, the monk who had made the accusation gets up and says, "I'm sorry. I've been foolish and have made a false accusation against Sāriputta. May he forgive me."

The Buddha's response is, "Yes, you have been foolish and you have made a false accusation but, having recognized your faults and wanting to make amends, you can grow in the Dhamma and Discipline." Then he turns to Sāriputta and says, "Sāriputta, forgive this foolish man before his head splits in seven pieces." Sāriputta says, "I certainly forgive him and may he forgive me for anything I have done."

I thought it was interesting how Sāriputta's immediate response was: "Somebody who has cultivated mindfulness of the body for as long as I have, and is so grounded in it, couldn't possibly give rise to unwholesome states and is well established in the quality of loving-kindness and compassion."

These are some reflections on mindfulness of the body and establishing a base. Perhaps we could go and do some walking meditation and then come back for a sitting. Of course, walking meditation is not any different than sitting, in the sense that when you're sitting, you're watching your breath and, when you're doing walking meditation, you're still paying attention to the whole body, but the primary focus is on the rhythm of the steps. You're pacing, walking a bit more slowly than normal or using whatever pace feels comfortable for establishing mindfulness.

Pay attention to the sensation of the right foot touching, rising, moving, and of setting that foot down. Left foot coming up, moving, setting down. Simply pace, paying attention to the rhythm of the walking, the sensation of touching the ground, the movement of the foot, and then the whole body. What's your posture like?

Again, it's not merely disembodied feet touching the pavement. It's the whole body connecting with the rhythm of the walking and paying attention to the posture. Holding your hands clasped, usually in front—it could be in back, but usually in front is a bit more comfortable—so that there is a composure to the posture. Keep your eyes downcast so that your gaze is about six feet in front. About twenty, twenty-five, thirty paces is appropriate, whatever is comfortable.

When you get to the end of the path and turn around, it's helpful to stop for a minute, to check and see: Am I here? Am I still present? Am I still with the walking? Then continue the walking. At the end of the path, stop for a minute because it's easy when the body is walking for the mind to wander off as well. So connect with present reality, make sure you are sustaining that connection with the posture and the continuity of mindfulness.

Introduction to Mettā Meditation

Loving-kindness is not separated from
what you are feeling in the body.

When we reflect on loving-kindness and use it as a meditation, it's good to reflect on its foundation. One of the ways that Ajahn Sumedho describes this is "not dwelling in aversion." That's a helpful way to look at loving-kindness.

In the Noble Eightfold Path, there is *sammā-saṅkappa*, right intention or right thought. There are three aspects of this: *nekkhamma-saṅkappa*, the aspect of renunciation or not drifting into sensuality; *abyāpāda-saṅkappa*, not thinking with ill will or aversion; and *avihiṃsa-saṅkappa*, thoughts of non-harming. The last two are often equated with loving-kindness and compassion.

For loving-kindness to arise, there have to be thoughts of non-ill will, non-aversion. These thoughts are fundamentally simple. We often think to ourselves, "I should be thinking these sublime thoughts of love for all beings, everywhere." But it's a great start if you can just not get averse to other beings. It's easier to begin this way as well. You can then encourage yourself along the way.

Encouraging ourselves is very important. That in itself is an act of loving-kindness, encouraging ourselves in something skillful. Bhante Guṇaratana tells a lovely story. He was going to teach in Europe, and when it was getting close to the time that he was to leave, the person who invited him called and asked him, "What do you teach?" He said, "I teach mindfulness. I teach *vipassanā*." And she said, "You don't teach loving-kindness do you? I hate loving-kindness!"

In actual fact, loving-kindness is a major foundation for Bhante G's teachings. The reason why the sponsor hated loving-kindness was she felt that she was supposed to have it for everybody. She had been through the Second World War and, being Jewish, had lost many family members and her culture. So she had the hope, "You aren't going to get me to do loving-kindness."

However, when you reflect on loving-kindness, you realize that not to dwell in aversion is an act of great kindness to yourself. The reality is that the very first person to receive any of the loving-kindness you are able to conjure up in your heart is you, whether it is directed to yourself or not. Classically, the way the instructions were set up from the time of the earliest commentaries on the Buddha's teachings, when loving-kindness meditation was structured and systematized, was to direct loving-kindness towards yourself. You establish loving-kindness towards yourself before going on to generate loving-kindness for somebody else.

This has a very strong psychological foundation. You can't really share anything until your cup is full, or at least until there is something in your cup. So you should direct attention to the cultivation and bring into being thoughts of loving-kindness towards yourself. We can complicate this with feelings of uncertainty, doubt, or guilt: "Maybe I shouldn't be doing it towards myself, because I'm not worthy."

One of the monks in Australia, Ajahn Brahmavaṃso, teaches people that if you can't start with yourself, start with anything that evokes a feeling of loving-kindness—a little puppy, a kitten, anything like that—because in reality, the cultivation of loving-kindness is not the repeating of the words and phrases. It's about the actual experience of loving-kindness, warmth, acceptance, openness—the feeling tone of the heart, including concern for the happiness of yourself and others. It's about generating that feeling.

In terms of meditation, it's directing attention to the feeling or emotion of kindness and well-wishing and then finding ways to support and shore that up, to allow it to become stable, suffuse your own being with it, and spread it out. That requires mindfulness and attention, which is one of the reasons why I'm only introducing loving-kindness on the afternoon of the second day of teaching.

It's important to see that loving-kindness has a context of the refuges, precepts, mindfulness, and attention to the body, as well as faith, confidence, and effort. It is necessary to cultivate and develop all the spiritual faculties. A particular skillful and wholesome quality then arises, which you can then draw your attention to, while shining it forth.

When loving-kindness has a stable base, you can allow it to shine more brightly. Then if, for some reason, the feeling fades, you won't say to yourself, "Oh, I've completely blown it. I came on a mettā retreat and I can't keep the mettā going at all." That's not really the point. The point is that there is a comprehensive spiritual path to be cultivated. Loving-kindness is an opportunity or an option that we can direct attention to and see where it goes. We bring attention to the different faculties of our spiritual cultivation in meditation and, having built that base, we can then recognize that there is an opportunity to home in on a particular mature emotion and allow it to come forward.

This is very powerful, useful, and healing, but it's also only one of many aspects of the meditation. It's not a matter of succeeding or failing: it's seeing the opportunity that we have of cultivating the path and then seeing what comes up when we direct attention to loving-kindness. We can set our intention to the cultivation of loving-kindness and then start to be flooded by memories of something very painful. Perhaps there can be a lot of fear or aversion mixed in, but we can then direct attention to non-aversion: "Can I not get hooked into aversion and ill will?" Any practice that opens doors into the heart might result in not being sure what you find there, but they're your own doors. It's learning what is behind these doors that is important.

Again, this is one of the reasons why it's so important to have the foundation of precepts, generosity, restraint, reflection, and investigation. This gives you the solidity and stability to be able to not be shaken by what appears out of the doorways of the mind. One of the popular images from Ajahn Chah's teaching is the pond in the forest and how many wonderful creatures come to drink at that pond. It's quite a benign image, with nice, little bunny rabbits and furry creatures, but that's not all that comes to the pond. Aggressive ones with big teeth might like to drink there, too. This is nature as it is, and the mind is nature. Recognizing that it's all a part of nature, nothing is a problem.

This is also a wholesome result of loving-kindness practice. As we cultivate loving-kindness more and become grounded in it, the perception that nothing is a problem becomes clearer and clearer, and we are always established in well-wishing.

It's not that we *need* to wish for others' happiness and well-being. This is just the way it is at a cellular level. This is the way the heart responds when it's not being self-protective, when it's not buying into its complications. We gain confidence in this. Doing loving-kindness as a practice makes this very conscious. As it is cultivated, it becomes second nature.

I think of Ajahn Chah as a stellar example of somebody with loving-kindness. People wanted to draw close to him because of that kindness. I remember once we were walking around Ajahn Chah's monastery, Wat Pah Pong, with Ajahn Liem, after Ajahn Chah had passed away or maybe around the end of his life. Ajahn Liem, an excellent monk and teacher, said, "Ajahn Chah had such loving-kindness. That's why so many people wanted to be with him, come close to him. That's why I've opted for equanimity." This loving-kindness creates a lot of work! People who have met Ajahn Liem know he has that air of equanimity. He's in the midst of everything and his attitude is, "Oh, it's just the world."

In consciously cultivating loving-kindness, we use phrases. One of the ways of doing the meditation is to use a phrase and then let it resonate for a bit—such as the phrase of sharing loving-kindness, "May I be well, happy, and peaceful." Set an intention of well-wishing and then allow it to resonate for a bit and settle in the body. Loving-kindness is not separated from what you are feeling in the body. Relax and settle. You are using the phrases as a meditation tool, a *parikamma*, a repetition that helps the mind to focus.

The articulation of loving-kindness in thought or verbalizing it helps you to see: this is the present moment. If this is the thought, then what's the feeling? You can then draw attention into the heart. What's the feeling? Relax, paying attention to the body and using the breathing to soften.

I'll do this as a guided meditation. Then it will be something you can use on your own as a practice, at your own speed. I will do it at the speed that I feel comfortable with when teaching a group, which doesn't necessarily mean that is how I do it when I'm on my own. To do the meditation, tune in to the body, paying attention to and relaxing your posture, allowing the breathing to settle deeply—tapping in to the rhythm of the breathing and planting a seed within that sphere of relaxation. Then pay attention to the feeling.

I can't emphasize enough that *mettā-bhāvanā*, the development of loving-kindness, is not about getting proficient at memorizing the lines or coming up with really neat new lines: "the revolutionary art of cultivating loving-kindness, new and improved!" Pay attention to the feeling and then allow that feeling to permeate, suffuse, and spread through the body, mind, and heart.

At the beginning there will just be little flickers of loving-kindness and the feeling that we associate with a sense of warmth, kindness, or loving attention. That's fine. Recognize how to nurture that. The way of nurturing it is using phrases that seem meaningful. When Jayantā asked me if there was anything she could bring, such as copies of different loving-kindness phrases, I said yes. Some of the phrases might resonate with you, and some might not. There is a whole array of different formulations. Become familiar with what actually resonates within the heart.

It's the nature of the mind that once you have something that works quite nicely and you use it for a while, the mind gets inured to it. It's then helpful to come at it from another angle and use other phrases, keeping it fresh.

The bringing up of the phrases is an act of mindfulness; being attentive and following a sequential pattern requires a certain mindfulness, consistency, and application of mind. That is part of the cultivation. Bringing up and sustaining loving-kindness takes patience in using and repeating the phrases and techniques.

When loving-kindness appears, it is of course important not to grab on to it. Don't take hold of this feeling of loving-kindness and desperately try to make it stable and steady. That is like taking a tiny little bird in your hand and squashing it. As with any other meditation object, you have to hold it very lightly, and if it stays, fine. It's like shoring or propping it up and allowing it to grow. It's very difficult to force that feeling.

As you direct attention to positive thoughts of well-being and well-wishing, it's important not to try to fend off any negative thoughts. If negative thoughts of irritation and aversion come in, establish the mind in non-ill will towards them. There is a whole series of discourses in which the Buddha is sitting in the forest and Māra, the evil one (Buddhism's Lucifer and the embodiment of the forces of darkness) comes and whispers in the Buddha's ear: "You're not really enlightened. It's just a cop out," or "You really should be taking more responsibility."

The Buddha's response is, "I know you, Māra." That's all it takes for Māra to pack up his gear; he's done for. It's the same for our own minds. The forces of Māra come whispering, "This is unbearable . . ." The response is, "I know you Māra." We don't have to destroy, annihilate, or get rid of the ill will. As soon as it's seen clearly, the forces of Māra have no ammunition or traction. There's nothing they can do.

This is a personification of what goes on in our own minds. If things come up in the mind, whether it's something we're really attracted to, want to distract ourselves with, or doubtful about, it's really helpful to say, "I know you Māra." And then bring constancy to the cultivation of loving-kindness or whatever meditation we are doing. Today we are using loving-kindness, but this really applies to our whole practice.

As you use the phrases, experiment with them. As you continue your practice, experiment and see what is helpful for sustaining the feeling of well-wishing. It's like lighting a fire. You have a lighter or a match, and then you have a small flame. You light some paper, get some kindling and some bigger wood, and you can build a bigger and bigger fire.

You do the same thing within the heart. You have a small flame of "May I be well." Just attend to that, nurture it, and protect it from the wind. Slowly get more fuel for that positive feeling. Start with a small spark and then allow it to gain momentum.

That's the quality we bring into the practice, that intention of nurturing, of protecting, of bringing into being something that is very wholesome, positive, and precious. Take care to allow yourself to do that. Sometimes we don't give ourselves the time or space simply to allow a feeling of warmth, vulnerability, care, or security to establish itself. It's a curious aspect of the human condition, but there it is. It's a great gift to be able to give ourselves that time and space.

I'm going to do a guided meditation using particular phrases for the sharing of loving-kindness. This is quite a classical way of doing it. The phraseology might not be classical, but the approach is classical in the sense of directing loving-kindness towards yourself, your parents, and your teachers—the people who are most *kammically* important and binding. Then start to spread it out to your family, friends, and then even those who are unfriendly because loving-kindness starts to be non-discriminative. Even those who are unfriendly—they're suffering, and we wish for them to be happy. Then extend loving-kindness out to all living beings without distinction.

Guided Meditation

Again, begin by settling into the posture, relaxing any tension you are feeling in the shoulders, around the eyes, the jaw. Allow the breath to settle into the abdomen, letting yourself be very comfortable. Allow a spaciousness in the mind. Then think the thought, "May I be well, happy, peaceful and prosperous." A sense of well-wishing toward yourself, emotionally and materially: "May no harm come to me. May no difficulties come to me. May no problems come to me."

On a certain level, we know that there is always going to be some difficulty, some problems in life. That's the way things are. But just set the wish, "May no harm come to me, no difficulties, no problems." Allow that sense of ease and well-being that comes when you do not have to deal with anything like that in the moment.

"May I always meet with success." I think I'd like to add a word to that: "May I always meet with *spiritual* success." The sense is, "I have the wish to cultivate that which is truly good." That's a spiritual aspiration. "May I have success in my spiritual endeavors." That's a true aspiration.

"May I have the patience, courage, understanding, and determination to meet and overcome inevitable difficulties, problems, and failures in life." That well-wishing encompasses the reality that there are difficulties and problems. There is always going to be some sort of failure or another, but may I have the qualities that will allow me to see those through. May I have patience.

Ajahn Chah once said, "I don't actually teach very much at all. I just teach people to be patient." That patience is courage, a willingness to be present with things, whether they are pleasant or unpleasant. There is a curiosity to want to understand and see things through, and a determination and willingness to stick with things.

I think all of us, if we've taken on spiritual practice and stuck with it for a long enough time—certainly I can vouch for the monastics—are all pretty stubborn, actually. We need to allow that stubbornness to become discerning determination. We have the opportunity to do something really skillful and wholesome and to stick with it. These are the qualities that allow us to let things pass through. That's an act of kindness. Allow it to be grounded in loving-kindness.

I'd like to repeat the phrases again. It's important that we don't just skip to "May everybody else receive loving-kindness." It's really important that we're willing to take the time to direct it towards ourselves and allow it to become established within our own hearts. "May I be well, happy, peaceful, and prosperous. May no harm come to me. May no difficulties come to me. May no problems come to me. May I always meet with spiritual success. May I have the patience, courage, understanding, and determination to meet and overcome inevitable difficulties, problems, and failures in life."

Then direct these thoughts of well-wishing, that sense of gratitude, to one's parents, particularly if they are still alive, but even if they've passed away. Even if you have had a difficult relationship with your parents, at least you've made it to this point. That's a big deal. "May my parents be well, happy, peaceful, and prosperous. May no harm come to them. May no difficulties come to them. May no problems come to them. May they always meet with spiritual success. May they always have the patience, courage, understanding, and determination to meet and overcome inevitable difficulties, problems, and failures in life."

Now direct attention of loving-kindness towards your teachers, whether it's teachers in worldly skills and knowledge or your spiritual teachers. We are able to cultivate a path of spiritual development because of our relationship to teachers that we have had and still have. It's an important connection to be grateful for and to honor and delight in. "May my teachers be well, happy, peaceful, and prosperous. May no harm come to them. May no difficulties come to them. May no problems come to them. May they always meet with spiritual success. May they also have the patience, courage, understanding, and determination to meet and overcome inevitable difficulties, problems, and failures in life."

Allow attention to be directed towards family, whether it's spouses, partners, children, aunts, uncles, cousins, nieces, nephews, or anyone we're related to by reason of *kamma*. "May my family be well, happy, peaceful, and prosperous. May no harm come to them. May no difficulties come to them. May no problems come to them. May they always meet with spiritual success. May they also have the patience, courage, understanding, and determination to meet and overcome inevitable difficulties, problems, and failures in life."

Allow the attention to broaden, encompassing your friends and friendly acquaintances: "May my friends be well, happy, peaceful, and prosperous. May no harm come to them. May no difficulties come to them. May no problems come to them. May they always meet with spiritual success. May they have the patience, courage, understanding, and determination to meet and overcome inevitable difficulties, problems, and failures in life."

Then we can bring to mind those whom we are neutral towards. We may have some acquaintance with them, but there is no strong feeling either way. "May those who are neutral to me be well, happy, peaceful, and prosperous. May no harm come to them. May no difficulties come to them. May no problems come to them. May they always meet with spiritual success. May they have the patience, courage, understanding, and determination to meet and overcome inevitable difficulties, problems, and failures in life."

Now allow your attention to include even those who we feel are unfriendly towards us, people we've had difficulty with or whom, in normal circumstances, we wouldn't think of in a kindly way. Recognize that we're all in the same boat of birth, aging, sickness, and death, and that they're worthy of our well-wishing, our kindness. "May those unfriendly to me be well, happy, peaceful, and prosperous. May no harm come to them. May no difficulties come to them. May no problems come to them. May they always meet with spiritual success. May they have the patience, courage, understanding, and determination to meet and overcome inevitable difficulties, problems, and failures in life."

Allow the heart to be non-discriminative, expansive, and unlimited in its wish towards all living beings. "May all living beings be well, happy, peaceful, and prosperous. May no harm come to them. May no difficulties come to them. May no problems come to them. May they always meet with spiritual success. May they have the patience, courage, understanding, and determination to meet and overcome inevitable difficulties, problems, and failures in life."

You can take the next period of sitting to work with the practice on your own, as feels comfortable, meaningful, or useful to you.

Questions and Answers

Let's begin the question-and-answer session. It looks like there is a veritable blizzard of questions. That's always encouraging.

Question: Can you speak a little bit about *samatha-vipassanā* and explain the difference between serenity and equanimity?

Answer: *Samatha-vipassanā* is actually a commentarial division. *Samatha* is about tranquility, *vipassanā* about insight. This has a scriptural basis to a certain extent, but as the commentaries tried to systematize the teachings and methodologies, there was a division into distinct realms and separate practices. Samatha includes concentration and tranquility practices. Vipassanā practices are insight techniques.

I tend to lean much more towards the earliest tradition. The Buddha himself didn't draw huge distinctions between the two. Also, my teacher, Ajahn Chah, didn't teach in a way that drew large distinctions between them. Oftentimes he said, "Samatha-vipassanā is kind of like a green mango and a ripe mango. Same mango, but it's a part of the process of ripening."

The aspects of concentration—settling the mind, unification, creating tranquility—are part of the same process of ripening. The reflective, investigative, contemplative aspects of the practice are part of the same spectrum of practice and training. They depend on each other. A proficiency in both of these aspects of training is required for the mind, the heart, to ripen in relinquishment and liberation.

There is a difference between serenity and equanimity. Serenity is often used as a translation for samatha (tranquility or peaceful abiding of the mind). This is more the result of a concentration and focusing practice.

Equanimity is a bit more nuanced in the sense that it is, first, a brahmavihāra, part of the spectrum of loving-kindness, compassion, sympathetic joy, and equanimity. These are sublime, lofty states of mind that result in a very refined state of consciousness. Equanimity is also an enlightenment factor. The seven factors of enlightenment taught by the Buddha are mindfulness, reflection on Dhamma, effort, joy, tranquility, concentration, and equanimity. Equanimity is also a factor of wisdom in the sense of the mind becoming very stable, steady, and unshakeable because of an abiding involving both emotion and wisdom. So equanimity is a bit more nuanced. Samatha is just the settling of the mind, the peacefulness of the mind, a peaceful abiding.

Q: Could you please explain the death process? What happens to us as we die or as the body dies? How quickly does rebirth occur? Is there anything in those last moments of that life that affects how we are reborn: our thoughts, our environment, how we are being cared for, our mature or not-so mature emotions, and so forth?

A: One of the things that is good to take into account is that when we think about the death process, we often think, "There I am, in my bed at home, surrounded by my family and loved ones, and then I mindfully pay attention to the death process." In reality, more often what happens is unpredictable, such as driving down the road at night, all of a sudden there are headlights coming straight at you, and it's, "Oh, shit!" That's the death process. Or it's completely out of your control: you are carted off to the hospital for some reason or other, they fill you full of tubes, and then you are wondering, "Well, this isn't how I wanted it."

We idealize how we think we are going to die. Death can come quickly, come slowly, it can come on our terms, it can come not on our terms at all—more often than not, that is what happens. So, the preparation for death is reflection and investigation on a day-to-day basis. One of the chants in the chanting book is called *abhiṇha-paccavekkhana*: things that are to be reflected upon again and again. The Buddha said we should be reflecting on these on a daily basis.

"I am of the nature to age; I have not gone beyond aging. I am of the nature to sicken; I have not gone beyond sickness. I am of the nature to die; I have not gone beyond dying. All that is mine, beloved, and pleasing, will become otherwise, will become separated from me. I am the owner of my *kamma*, heir to my *kamma*, born of my *kamma*, related to my *kamma*, abide supported by my *kamma*. Whatever *kamma* I shall do, for good or for ill, of that I will be the heir."

The reflections on aging, sickness, death, impermanence, separation, and being the owner of our *kamma* are preparation for the death process. It is exceedingly important to challenge our perceptions, illusions of control, and the assumptions about how long we are going to live. If we've been practicing for a bit, we usually get it that we have to die at some point in time, but it's usually "off in the future." There are so many different ways of dying.

What happens to us as we die? As we die, there is a breakdown of the physical body, of the processes that sustain life, and on a certain level, of the mind itself. Not in the sense of "we all fall apart and go bonkers," but there is the breakdown of what we conceive of as "my mind and my thoughts." We prop that up through our whole life and identify with the thoughts, memories, and perceptions. That starts to unravel.

If what you have done is spend your life identifying with thoughts, feelings, perceptions, and memories, then it's going to be confusing because it's just natural that these unravel. Reflections in the morning chanting include, "The body is impermanent, feelings are impermanent, perceptions are impermanent, mental formations are impermanent, consciousness is impermanent; the body is not self, feelings are not self, perceptions are not self, mental formations are not self, consciousness is not self." These are extraordinarily important reflections to investigate and to take on board, so that you are not identifying with and building your home in these impermanent, not-self phenomena, as is the habit of human beings.

Rebirth generally takes place fairly quickly. The Theravadin doctrine is that it's an instantaneous rebirth. Doctrinal positions were generated historically after the Buddha passed away. The various schools of Buddhism, such as the Theravadins, had particular positions that they took, and one of them was this instantaneous rebirth. There is some scriptural basis for that, but I think one of the wonderful things about Theravadin scriptures is that they kept everything. As the name itself, "the way of the elders," indicates, they tried to keep everything. They were the conservative element.

So within the scriptures, you can also have things that contradict that. The *antarābhava*, the in-between becoming, is a state the Buddha talked about. There is also a discourse in which the Buddha compared the state to a fire being blown by the wind. The wind picks up the flame and pushes it somewhere else, which could be near or far away. The Buddha compared that to the desire, the degree of *taṇhā* and identification, that impels the mind to rebirth.

In general, I don't think it's as neat and tidy as the ancient Theravadins put it, instantaneous rebirth, or as neat and tidy as the Tibetans put it, at forty-nine days, or that it's like this, this, or this. I don't think anything is neat and tidy. But there are these processes by which rebirth is generated. Rebirth is generated by identification, attachment, state of mind, and the degree of clarity and calmness within the mind.

That is why within Thai tradition, there is emphasis on people attending to a person who is dying: supporting them, making sure they're comfortable and feeling a sense of ease, physically, emotionally, and spiritually. Trying to remind them by chanting, speaking to them, meditating around them, spreading loving-kindness around the sick bed—these are very supportive ways of creating a wholesome mental state. It does have an effect when the mind is in a wholesome state and is clear.

Those transitions are also a time of opportunity as well, of very deep letting go. "Right, I've heard this. 'I am of the nature to die.' I've heard this before." The important thing is then being able to turn to relinquishment from a place of calm. It's possible. That is why the support is there and is culturally encouraged.

In all cultures, there tends to be a washing of the body, a ritual both for the people who are alive and for the person who has died so that they can make the transition with peace and relinquishment. This is important.

There are also those who have built up unskillful habits over a lifetime. One of Ajahn Chah's former monks asked him about working with death and dying, and working with people like that to give them the opportunity for a wholesome rebirth. Ajahn Chah had his cane beside him and, poked the former monk in the chest, knocked him over, pushed him on the ground and said, "buddho, buddho." Ajahn Chah was saying that the time of death can be painful and very difficult, and if somebody hasn't done the work beforehand, it's not that easy. So it's important to prepare throughout our lives. His Holiness the Dalai Lama was once asked what the basis of his spiritual practice was, and he said, "I practice dying."

Q: As a guilt-ridden American, I can't quite comprehend how to respond without guilt when I have caused harm, even inadvertently. Could you walk through the non-guilt-oriented mental process of a person who has harmed or caused inconvenience to someone else? I'm thinking of the monk who falsely accused Sāriputta. If that were me, I would practically have to leave the sangha out of embarrassment and shame.

A: It's essentially answered in the way the Buddha responded when the monk made his confession—"I falsely accused Sāriputta"—and then asked for forgiveness. The Buddha said, "It's recognizing one's faults as faults, one's unskillful action as unskillful action and wishing to make amends: that is growth in the Noble One's Discipline." That in itself is the difference. Recognizing that we all make mistakes, whether it's intentionally or unintentionally, we have the opportunity to reestablish ourselves in that which is skillful, appropriate, in accordance with truth.

Nobody is exempt. Remorse, from a Buddhist perspective, says, "I really missed my shot on that and that was unskillful," and there is an impetus to change. In Pali there is the word *hiri-ottappa*: *hiri* is a sense of conscience or embarrassment toward an action done in the past; *ottappa* is a concern for future wrong-doing. It's interesting when you say it in English because early translators used shame and fear of wrongdoing, and what comes up in our minds is that these are heavy, negative states, whereas in the Pali language, these are actually wholesome mental states in the way that mental states are categorized.

In Pali it's called *kusala*. Intrinsic to *kusala* or a wholesome mental state is a sense of well-being, clarity, and discernment. It's having the clarity to recognize, "That is really unbecoming and not in accord with how I really want to be, so it would be better for me to step back from that," rather than, "Oh, my god, I did this and what are people going to think of me? I can't show my face around here anymore." That spins around "me": me and the problems I've created; me and my awfulness. That in itself is the problem.

The recognition of that which is unskillful has a very wholesome, protective quality. Also, in the Pali language, when that quality of conscience or concern toward wrongdoing is described, the underlying state of the mind regarding hiri is one of respect for ourselves, in the sense that we do not want to do something that would be inappropriate or not in accord with our values and deepest intentions. Ottappa arises out of respect for others because we recognize that as human beings, we're in the same boat of being subject to birth-aging-sickness-death. We have a mixture of wholesome and unwholesome qualities. There is a fundamental respect for other beings and therefore, we don't want to harm anybody else either. Both qualities are underpinned by an underlying respect.

The quality of guilt does not give oneself due respect. It undermines our own wholesome qualities. It's really interesting to reflect on the Buddha's statement that the recognition of our unskillful actions is a sign of growth in the Noble One's teaching and training. It's the actions that speak louder than the perception of individuality.

That's what tends to govern our sense of who we are: the perception of individuality rather than a recollection of the intentions and actions that we rely on. What do we do on a habitual basis? How do we make our decisions? There are very few Buddhist meditators whose lives are committed to stealing, dishonesty, harming, and violence; it's pretty rare. But the perception is not in accord with the real actions; rather, the perception is often driven by guilt.

So it's important to be able to separate that out, to say, "Well actually, I'm committed to integrity, to that which is good. I'm going to shrink back from things that are unskillful." Also, anybody can make a mistake and miss their shot. A person has the opportunity to recognize that and reestablish him or herself in what is skillful.

There are several occasions in the scriptures where we might think that the Buddha really messed up. It doesn't come across that the Buddha was agonized with guilt and struggling. It's more like, "That didn't work! I'll try it this way instead." One of the things that is very helpful to do when recognizing that we have missed our shot is asking for forgiveness and seeking reconciliation. It's not that difficult to do, and it's very healing.

Q: How would you describe the *jhāna* states, and do you teach this kind of meditation?

A: That's pretty extensive. The *jhāna* states are internal states of stability and composure that are a basis for very bright states of consciousness. These are states the Buddha encourages because they lead to an energizing and a clarity of the mind that allows seeing things in their true nature. They are a very skillful tool.

I tend to follow Ajahn Chah's way of teaching. Ajahn Chah would describe the jhāna states as a process of letting go. To the extent that you are willing to let go, the mind settles very stably and steadily. I think that is very helpful because oftentimes there can be a tremendous amount of desire generated for attaining the jhānas and comparing yourself to those who do attain the jhānas. Maybe you do attain the jhānas, but then further comparing occurs; it goes on and on. Recognize that the refined states of consciousness are most easily approached and accessed when we are able to keep letting go of those aspects of the mind that are obstructive. As we keep doing that, the mind settles.

Q: When there is a lot of pain in the body, it is difficult to maintain right effort. Yet sometimes, through patient endurance, the pain lessens. Can you speak about right effort and the connection between right effort and *samādhi*?

A: It's good to refresh our memory as to what right effort actually is. When we conceive of right effort, we use the word "effort," and of course effort is about doing, struggling: getting out there and energetically being assiduous and diligent, which is sometimes good.

But the way the Buddha defines right effort is effort for decreasing unwholesome mental states that have arisen. Effort for the preventing of unwholesome mental states that have yet to arise is also right effort. Effort for the bringing into being of wholesome states that have not yet arisen is right effort. And effort for the maintaining of wholesome states that have arisen is right effort.

It might sound a bit convoluted, but it's a very clear description, once you get your mind around it. When the Buddha defines it, it's all about actual mental states. Right effort is not about how diligent we appear externally or how much we flog ourselves. It's about attending to the quality of the mind—wholesome or un-wholesome—and how we relate to the unwholesome or unskillful states: whether we support them, buy into them, or exacerbate them, at the expense of undermining the wholesome.

Similarly with wholesome states: how do we encourage those wholesome mental states, those bright states of mind? How do we maintain them, without clamping down, shutting down, or worry-ing? That worrying is in itself an unwholesome mental state.

In dealing with pain, it's helpful to pay attention and see the difference between the physical sensation and the mental elabora-tions around the pain. The physical sensation of pain is oftentimes telling us something like, "I'm tired. I want out of here." Something is stressed and pain is a warning, trying to get our attention. There are many levels to the physical side: some of it is bearable; some of it may not be necessary to bear and needs to be adjusted, dealt with, or ameliorated in some way.

On the mental level, what is the reaction, what is being added, what is the level of fear or aversion? Pain can be very threatening. It can also be very useful. It definitely gets our attention. There is an immediacy there, so we can even use pain to challenge the mind and the assumptions that we have, bringing a certain urgency to practice.

There's no single response. We need to be balanced. We need to see what is a genuine call of distress that needs to be heeded and what we can just be patient with, bearing with the pain and direct-ing attention to the mind itself. Sometimes with pain we can simply direct attention to the physical sensation of the pain. Sometimes we can absorb into the pain and the mind can be very, very peaceful. We can be inside the sensation and find that the mind becomes very cool and bright.

There are many ways of responding. It's a very interesting as-pect of the practice. Having physical bodies, we are always going to experience some sort of pain. We can learn a lot about how much we expect, how much we push, or how much we worry or fear, through seeing our reactions to pain. It's something that is very natural. Having pain is a natural part of the human condition, and it's important to learn how to deal with it skillfully.

I think one of the main things is gaining confidence that pain can be worked with and that there is a point at which the appropriate way of working with it is to back off, rest, or do something about it. At other times, we can just go into the pain. For many years of my early monastic life, pain, illness, and injury were fairly constant features of my meditation. I had the opportunity and had to use it. I had to become familiar with pain, and I find that that has held me in good stead.

Q: What is loving-kindness? What is the body and mind's experience when I feel mettā for myself and others?

A: I think everybody is going to experience it in a slightly different way. There is not a formulaic way that you should experience loving-kindness. There is a general parameter at the base of loving-kindness, which is dwelling in non-aversion, to put it in negative terms.

Oftentimes Western culture casts things in idealistic ways. We are very good at ideals: ideally, what would be the perfect expression of loving-kindness? That's what we try to get, and we can drive ourselves nuts doing this.

I think it's helpful to begin with a less idealistic basis: dwelling in non-aversion. It's the absence of aversion, of ill will. Recognizing that, we have something fairly tangible to work with. There is an experience and a recognition because we don't dwell in aversion all the time, do we? We don't spend our whole lives in ill will and grumpiness towards the whole world.

We then build on that in a more positive sense. When it's translated into the Thai language, it is expressed as a well-wishing, wishing oneself and others well. There is a recognition of what we would appreciate, of what others would appreciate: that sense of well-being. I think that is a very useful perception of loving-kindness.

Sometimes the English language is loaded with our cultural baggage: "How can I be loving towards myself and all living beings? I don't love everybody." Well, sometimes you don't even like them, but you can wish them well. You can establish that wish for your own well-being and for others' well-being. You don't even have to like people to do that. I think that is casting it into a light that is practical and realistic.

Sometimes it's good to use words that are unfamiliar to us. Bhante Guṇaratana plays with language: loving friendliness or an appreciative friendliness. It's not a word that we use all the time, but it's trying to convey a particular feeling. That kind of well-wishing or appreciative friendliness is the mental state. Internally, within the mind, there is a warmth, spaciousness, non-contention, a concern for others' well-being.

Then, of course, there will be a physical relaxation. Aversion, ill will, contention—these have their attendant feelings of agitation and tightening within the body. Physically, with loving-kindness, we will feel a sense of ease, spaciousness, and settledness. Within the heart there will be a similar sense of openness. There will be space for yourself and for others.

So these are some reflections. I enjoy the questions. I never quite know what is going to come out when people present a question. It's interesting to me as well.

The Five Hindrances

By fully pervading the body and mind with this
quality of loving-kindness we can draw back
from the five hindrances.

As we develop meditation, whether it's mettā-bhāvanā or other kinds of meditation, we always have to develop skill in dealing with what are called the hindrances, *nīvaraṇa* in Pali. It's something that we need to be attentive to, not just in meditation, but in daily life and our interactions with people. Whether we're walking, sitting, standing, or lying down, we need to be aware of how these hindrances overwhelm or obscure the mind.

The hindrances that the Buddha pointed to are sensual desire, ill will, sloth and torpor, restlessness and worry, and skeptical doubt. These undermine the goodness, steadiness, and clarity of the mind, so it's important that we become aware of something as a hindrance, particularly in the context of cultivation of the meditations on loving-kindness. When ill will, anger, aversion, irritation, and negativity arise, there should be an immediate flag going up in the mind that says, "Aha, this is a hindrance." Not, "That schmuck. How could they do that?" That's the immediate belief in a construct of negativity, rather than a sense of, "Oh, this is a hindrance; now how do I deal with it?"

As with other aspects of meditation, one of the important foundations of dealing with the hindrances is tuning in to the body. Recognizing, what does the body feel like when there is sensual desire? Where do you feel it? How does it make the body feel: the excitement, the anticipation, the leaning into the hope of gratification?

What does the body feel like with ill will, negativity, and aversion: the feeling of being on edge and tensing that energizes us? Of course it's not a very wonderful kind of energy, but sometimes it temporarily feels better than nothing if you're looking for something to get energized with. Sometimes it seems that there's nothing better than a good rant to clear out the pipes, but that leaves debris everywhere.

Sloth and torpor: what does it feel like in the body? What's the general tone—listlessness, dullness? Restlessness and worry: the agitation you feel isn't just a mental event; the body is involved as well. Doubt: that uncertainty, hesitation, inability to move forward, that feeling of pulling back.

These are things that we feel in the body. We learn how to be attentive to the experience of the hindrances as a whole body/mind process. As we cultivate mindfulness of breathing and mindfulness of the body, things start to become a bit clearer. You sense that this is a hindrance rather than feeling out of sorts and uncomfortable and then looking for something to blame, either externally or by blaming yourself. You can reflect, "Oh, this is what I'm feeling." Work with that; breathe through it, bringing attention to the feeling with clear awareness.

Bring up something skillful and wholesome to work with. One of the discourses of the Buddha begins with Ānanda visiting a group of nuns. There is an exchange concerning the nuns' practice, and the nuns are making particularly good progress in their cultivation of meditation and training. Ānanda tells the Buddha, and the Buddha gives a discourse, approving the practice and adding that in the cultivation of mindfulness and meditation, it is necessary to direct the mind to something uplifting (S 47.10).

When the mind is scattered, diffused, or overwhelmed by dullness or torpor, direct the attention to something that is uplifting and pleasurable. The word in Pali is *pasādaniya-nimitta*: a sign of that which is pleasurable or satisfying.

We are directing attention to mettā-bhāvanā. That's a particularly pleasurable sign and object of attention to direct the mind to. This isn't done only to overcome ill will and aversion. It also can be very helpful with sloth and torpor, when the mind is dull. When we direct the mind to something pleasurable, the mind can take interest in it. Usually we get trapped in sloth and torpor because we are not sufficiently interested in something as neutral as the breath, but the object of loving-kindness is very pleasurable. Or with restlessness and worry, we can have a mind that is fidgety, worried, or anxious about this or that. The mind will latch on to anything because it's quite happy to worry about anything. But give the mind something pleasurable, and it can take some satisfaction in hanging out with that. Hang out with loving-kindness, and let it churn. If the mind is going to churn, let it churn with something skillful.

Sometimes people pick up a strongly adversarial approach to dealing with unwholesome, unwanted states of mind. In Buddhist teachings, the language can often take on a warrior-like tone. The Buddha was from the warrior caste and did use those images, but they aren't what he used all the time.

This is a very good example of the different ways that the Buddha approached the practice. Sometimes it's solely to be mindful. It's all going to work out; we just have to be mindful. All we need to do is gently bring the mind back to the object as an impartial observer. It should be noted, though, that the impartial observer is often a fallacy. We have our issues and agendas going all the time, whether we're aware of them or not. Part of the function of our practice is to understand those agendas.

Another approach is to bring attention consciously to something wholesome, skillful, pleasurable, and satisfying to the mind. On a certain level you know that doubt, wavering, and uncertainty are unskillful, but it's hard to convince the doubtful and wavering mind that loving-kindness is a good thing. You've got to work at it.

However, we need to be a bit circumspect. Feeding sensual desire with pleasurable objects is not a good idea; we are pretty good at that already. The appropriate way to address the tendency to sensual desire is to take it to another level. Instead of fixating on that which seems gratifying and pleasurable, realize, "Oh, there's so much suffering in this." Focus on loving-kindness and realize the kindest thing is not being trapped in sensual desire's illusion of pleasure and gratification.

The hindrances are a very fruitful realm for investigation, and overcoming them is a necessary foundation to lay for our practice. As we continue to cultivate, we need to be more and more skilled and quick at noticing: "Is that a hindrance? Is that an obstruction to that which is truly skillful?"

In another discourse, the Buddha points to the hindrances as being the fuel or nourishment for ignorance, *avijjā*. Ignorance, or not knowing the true nature of things, is the ground that all suffering arises out of. But that ignorance is not something that is immutable and indivisible, or a fixed aspect of the mind. It comes into being fed and nourished by certain conditions; the conditions that feed and nurture it are the five hindrances. If we are working with the five hindrances, we are very directly undermining that fundamental tendency towards avijjā, the lack of true knowledge and awareness.

As we practice through the day, doing sitting and walking meditation, be aware if a hindrance is present. "This particular thought, mood, perception, or feeling—could it be a hindrance?"

If it is, work with it. Ground it in the awareness of the body. When the Buddha describes the hindrances, he points out that when we're able to relinquish and let go of them, the mind is able to become more peaceful and settled. When we're able to relinquish the hindrance, joy, a sense of well-being, and satisfaction come up in the mind.

The Buddha gives images to illustrate this. He compares one who is overwhelmed by the hindrance of sensual desire to someone in debt. With sensual desire, there's always something hanging over you. When one is in debt there's always a sense of concern, so the mind isn't able to come to a place of ease. But when one has paid off one's debts, there's a sense of happiness, well-being, and joy that arises quite naturally. I think anybody who has finally paid off a mortgage thinks, "Wow, that feels so good." There is a sense of well-being and happiness that arises when sensual desire is abandoned and let go of.

Ill will is compared to somebody who is sick and has a fever. Food doesn't agree with him or her; nothing tastes good. As long as there is fever or illness, one feels out of sorts and uncomfortable, but when the sickness goes away, food tastes good and the world looks better again. A sense of happiness and well-being arises. The relinquishing and abandoning of ill will and aversion feels good.

Sloth and torpor, the dullness and drowsiness that overtake the mind, the Buddha compares to somebody who is in prison. When someone is put in prison, he or she doesn't have access to family or resources. There is a great sense of loss and suffering, but if the person is released from prison, property is restored, and connections with family reestablished, then he or she would feel extremely happy. There would be a sense of ease and well-being. Similarly, a sense of ease and well-being comes to one who is able to relinquish and abandon sloth and torpor.

The Buddha compares restlessness and worry to slavery. Slaves aren't able to go where they want or do what they want; they're not their own masters. If they were granted the freedom to go where they want and do what they want, they would feel happiness and well-being. It's the same way with the relinquishing of restlessness and worry. There is a tremendous sense of well-being if we realize that, having been a slave to restlessness, agitation, and worry, we are no longer worrying about something and in particular, we are not worrying about what the next thing to worry about is. To be able to put all that down and say, "There's just this body and this mind. There's this peace and awareness"—that's a different world.

Skeptical doubt, the Buddha compares to somebody who has property and possessions and who must travel through a desert or wilderness fraught with danger and robbers. If that person makes a safe passage through that desert or wilderness and gets to the destination with all property intact, he or she would experience joy and well-being. In the same way, when we are trapped in doubt, everything is fraught with danger, difficulty, and uncertainty; we are always wondering what is going to happen. If we relinquish that doubt, a sense of safety, refuge, and certainty arises.

There are many tools to use in working with these hindrances, but particularly during this retreat, please experiment with the application of loving-kindness. See how it's able to work as a means for undermining the hindrances. A sense of wholesomeness is intrinsic to loving-kindness. These are very beautiful states of mind. We can direct attention to loving-kindness and have confidence that this is a wholesome state of mind.

In the cultivation of more refined states of mind, as we relinquish the hindrances, the mind has a sense of brightness and stability. In the classical description of the first jhāna, the mind is withdrawn from sensual desires and unwholesome states of mind. Through the strength of that withdrawal, that delighting in seclusion from the agitation of sensual desire and from unwholesome states of aversion, ill will, doubt, restlessness, sloth, and torpor, the mind is able to settle.

We need to work at it to a certain extent. One of the descriptions that the Buddha gives is a bathman or a bathman's apprentice. In the Buddha's time they used a kind of clay for soap. You would take that ball of clay and wet it, knead it, and permeate and pervade, suffuse and fill that ball of clay, so that it's not too wet but the moisture completely pervades it. It doesn't drip and the consistency is very even. That's what you would use to rub against yourself if you were in a bath in the Buddha's time.

The meditator does the same thing with his or her body and mind. It's interesting that the Buddha points to the body. The meditator permeates and pervades, suffuses and fills the body with that delight in seclusion from sensual desire and unwholesome states. Attend to that feeling of seclusion, so that the mind is able to be present with the breath as it comes in and goes out of the body, as the body is sitting and relaxing. Fully permeating and pervading, suffusing and filling the breath, body, and mind with this quality of loving-kindness, drawing back from and relinquishing the five hindrances.

This is a present-moment practice. As you breathe in, there is a sense of permeating and pervading, suffusing and filling. As you breathe out, allow loving-kindness, the thoughts and feeling of well wishing, kindness, and warmth, to fill the body and mind.

If any hindrances arise, if there's any sensual desire, ill will, sloth and torpor, restlessness, or doubt, rather than seeing it as an enemy coming to attack and then gearing up to annihilate and destroy it, come from a base of loving-kindness: "How do I work with this? This is not to my benefit or well-being. What's a skillful way of relinquishing this? What's a skillful way of letting this go?" From that place, you can be as innovative as you want.

The classic advice for relinquishing sensual desire is the contemplation of the unattractive nature of the body. Oftentimes this contemplation is picked up with aversion, attending to the repugnant nature of the body. Why does it have to be like that? With loving-kindness you can say, "What's the point in this constant attraction to something that is always breaking down? It's never comfortable. Why do I keep trying to make it happy? Give it up." There is a kindness there. "Oh, okay, I can let that go." Then what is left in the mind is very bright.

With aversion and ill will, rather than being fearful, approach it with a sense of kindness: "This aversion, this ill will, why do I set myself up in opposition to everything? Why do I keep getting into arguments with it?" Even if you actually win the argument, there is still a resonance of having got into an argument with yourself, a petty squabble that you have maintained in your mind. "I can let that go."

Bring a sense of kindness to working with sloth and torpor. Sometimes we can get frustrated with sloth and torpor when the mind is dull, or we get very idealistic, thinking we should be able to sit and not have these intrusions of dullness. I think one of the things that is important to understand is that loving-kindness is not acquiescing to everything and saying everything is fine: "This sloth and torpor, isn't it lovely, wonderful?" or "That aggressive, obnoxious person, isn't he nice?" No, we don't have to acquiesce. But we don't have to get caught up in aversion, don't have to get trapped by the negativity.

So, we conserve a lot of energy by not fighting with sloth and torpor and instead recognizing, "What's a skillful way of working with this?" Sometimes it's a real kindness, rather than idealistically sitting and struggling, just to get up and stand. Go and do some walking meditation. Sit with your eyes open. "Sit with our eyes open? Do real meditators do that?" Well, why not? A very simple thing can give energy. Sitting with our eyes open can energize. We can pass through the period of sloth and torpor; it's actually fairly simple. But we do have to have kindness for ourselves to allow that, and we tend not to.

With restlessness and worry, it's helpful to tune in to the body. When the mind is restless, it's moving around, looking for something, *anything*. So permeate and pervade, suffuse and fill the body with the quality of loving-kindness. Breathe in and out, tuning in to the rhythm and the feeling of the energy through the body. Even if it's a restless energy, allow and be very conscious of permeating and pervading, suffusing and filling. Turn your attention to non-desire and step away from any unwholesome states, negativity, and aversion.

Find a place in the body that does feel comfortable. Then find an object that is pleasurable or satisfying, pasādaniya-nimitta. Maybe your chest or stomach is restless. Well, what about your hands? Can you just relax your hands? Can you make that a pleasurable sensation? Pick a spot and see that you can suffuse that particular area with a feeling of well-being and seclusion from the unwholesome. From that you have a base, and you can work on that to pervade the other areas of the body.

We are working in accord with that image of the bathman. It's a lovely image and very much body-based. And of course we do have a mind with this body as well. That is, we can affect the mind directly without getting entangled in it. Sometimes, seclusion is from the mind itself.

The mind goes off on a particular tangent, say, doubt. It's doubting about this, uncertain about that. Well, why do we have to make a decision? Why do we even have to have a particular opinion or a view about whether something is right or wrong? There is just this breath; there's just this sensation of the body, breathing in, breathing out. This itself is a great act of kindness.

Use the theme of the five hindrances and the application of loving-kindness, not simply as a theory or a mental state. Work it in and see how it pervades the rest of your practice. It's not just about meditation. It isn't as if you come into the meditation hall and the five hindrances appear only then. This is a life skill; get familiar with this. Also, the more skillful you are at becoming aware of how the five hindrances work and how you can relinquish them, then when you do come to sit, the more the mind is able to settle more quickly. So I offer that for reflection today.

The Karaṇīya-Mettā Sutta

The Buddha has laid it out quite clearly.
There is an intrinsic well-being that comes
from aligning ourselves with the skillful.

Yesterday, I introduced a method for the cultivation of loving-kindness using the phrases: "May I be well, happy, peaceful. May no harm come to me. May no difficulties come to me. May no problems come to me. May I always meet with spiritual success. May I have the patience, courage, understanding, and determination to meet and overcome inevitable difficulties, problems, and failures in life."

Then we used those same phrases to generate the recollection of loving-kindness towards parents, teachers, family, friends, those who are unfriendly, and then all living beings. I think the use of phrases is a helpful reminder to try to direct attention to a particular feeling. The feeling of loving-kindness is the object of meditation in this practice: the actual feeling, an emotional tone within the heart. That is what we are trying to generate, support, and sustain. As we direct attention, it's like trying to enter into and abide in that feeling, allowing it to establish itself.

I think it's also quite important in terms of the cultivation of loving-kindness that we recall this *mettā-nimitta*, the sign of loving-kindness. Find a place where that feeling of mettā begins to establish itself and then protect it. Then use the different phrases to try to support, nurture, and hold loving-kindness in a skillful way so that it can grow and expand.

Sometimes there is a problem with language: directing attention to parents and teachers isn't like taking loving-kindness and beaming it off this way and that way, shooting it out and radiating it. It's much more the sense of beginning with what might be a little spark and allowing the heart to be a vessel for loving-kindness. What we do is then expand that vessel, expand that sphere of loving-kindness, so that it includes parents, family, teachers, friends, and ultimately, all living beings.

Alternatively, it's establishing that base of loving-kindness, that mettā-nimitta, stabilizing it, nurturing it, and then inviting parents, teachers, and friends into it. Allow them to come into that sphere, include them so that the base of loving-kindness is right here, within this body and mind, in the present moment. This is where the base of loving-kindness is—then allow that to include other beings, inviting and expanding it so that it's not excluding anything.

This is thus a different approach in terms of stabilizing the concentration and using it as a meditation that provides a solid anchor within the heart. It's quite important, this shift of perspective to having a stable vessel of loving-kindness that then expands, allowing it to include all of these other beings we associate with. It's never divorced or separated from the loving-kindness that is established toward yourself. That is the base that you are always returning to and depending on: "May I be well, happy, peaceful. May no harm come to me. May no difficulties come to me. May no problems come to me. May I always meet with spiritual success. May I have the patience, courage, understanding, and determination to meet and overcome inevitable difficulties, problems, and failures in life."

It's always grounded in respect, kindness, and well-wishing toward yourself. That's not selfish. It's the most practical reality, to be able to look after yourself so that you have the resources to be able to support others.

Over these days, I'll introduce a few different methodologies, options, and kinds of phraseology. What rings true for you? What feels meaningful?

Today we will address the Buddha's words on loving-kindness, which is one of the chants that we do. It's probably the most famous expression of loving-kindness that the Buddha taught. The formula of directing loving-kindness towards yourself, parents, teachers, and friends is probably the most common structure. However, this particular chant is the most well-known teaching on loving-kindness in the suttas.

I've heard a couple of different Pali scholars who are fluent in Pali, Bhikkhu Bodhi and Bhante Guṇaratana, say that this is the most beautiful discourse in terms of the scriptural Pali language. There is not a spare word anywhere; it's all perfect. Of course, in trying to get things into English, you try your best, and there are many different translations. The beauty of the Internet is that you can find a half-dozen different translations of the *Karaṇīya-Mettā Sutta*.

One of the striking things, given that this is the Buddha's best-known discourse on loving-kindness, is that it is about a third of the way into the sutta before the Buddha even mentions loving-kindness. I think this is great, in the sense that loving-kindness is to be cultivated but that there is also that which should be done to get to that point. We need to be skilled in goodness and know the path of peace. "Let them be able and upright, straightforward and gentle in speech."

This is not just a mental phenomenon. We can't just grab a feeling of loving-kindness out of the ether of our mental states and hold on to it. No. It arises out of our actions and speech. This is the ground that we need to be attending to: the sense of our actions being able and upright, our speech being straightforward and direct.

When we chant the recollection of the Sangha the same word occurs: *uju*, direct, straight, upright, practicing directly. Be straightforward in speech, direct, but also gentle. There is a vivid idiom in the scriptural language: "Attacking each other with verbal daggers." Here's another one: "Someone born with an axe in their mouth." Speech can be just as harsh, cutting, and devastating as action, so it's important to be gentle as well as straightforward in speech.

The quality of being "humble and not conceited": there is a softness and a harmonious quality that arises in the human condition when somebody has humility and is not carrying around conceits of their importance and worth. "Contented and easily satisfied": similarly, in terms of being able to harmonize with each other in the human community, the sense of contentment and being easily satisfied is one that allows us to blend with each other. If we're discontented and difficult to satisfy, with constant demands, whether they are material or emotional, we're always walking on eggshells. It's difficult to get along. Again, there is an idiom from the scriptural language: "blending like milk and water."

One discourse comes to mind immediately (M 128). The scenario is that the Buddha has left the community because he has become fed up. The monks were arguing and refusing to listen to his advice. He went to a forest where a few other monks were living. One was his cousin, Anuruddha. The Buddha arrives and asks them, "Are you living harmoniously? Are you living blending like milk and water?" That's an image that is used to indicate that the sense of being contented and easily satisfied is a source of inner well-being as well as outer well-being.

"Unburdened with duties and frugal in their ways": not having too many things on our plate, not taking on more than we can handle. Living in simple ways: these are ways that allow us to have ease within the heart that can then be translated into a cultivation of a mature emotion like loving-kindness. "Peaceful and calm, wise and skillful": these are all qualities to be reminding ourselves of, in the sense of bringing them into our daily lives, qualities of calm and discernment. Making decisions, not according to our preferences or our ideals, but by asking: "What is truly skillful, wholesome, and beneficial? What is neither beneficial nor skillful, what is being driven either by your own biases or by the biases of the society around you?"

The Buddha defines that which is skillful as that which inherently leads to happiness, peace, and a freedom from the defilements and obscurations. What is unskillful, its opposite, is that which is associated with suffering, with *dukkha*. It's agitated, turbulent, and associated with greed, hatred, and delusion.

Asking, "What is really beneficial and skillful?" is helpful in making decisions, rather than, "Do I like it? Do I not like it? What is that person going to think? What's the popular notion within this particular group of people?" The Buddha has laid it out quite clearly. There is an intrinsic well-being that comes from aligning ourselves with the skillful.

"Not proud and demanding in nature. Let them not do the slightest thing that the wise would later reprove." If we wish to take into account and worry about what somebody is going to think, let's take the standards of somebody who is really wise and use that as a sounding board.

"Wishing in gladness and in safety, may all beings be at ease." The scriptural Pali is, *sukhino vā khemino hontu, sabbe sattā bhavantu sukhitattā. Sukhino* is happy, with gladness and well-being: may they be happy; may they experience well-being. *Khemino* is safety, security, stability, freedom from any kind of threat. *Sabbe sattā bhavantu sukhitattā*: may all beings bring this quality of happiness and well-being into being; may they be at ease.

Establish that wish, that thought, that aspiration. The Buddha then encourages us to expand that. "Whatever living beings there may be; whether they are weak or strong, omitting none; the great or the mighty, medium, short, or small." Weak or strong is not just a physical attribute. It could also be a social attribute, whether they are powerful or disadvantaged. It's not just whether they are ninety-eight-pound weaklings or Mr. Universe. It's much more regarding any physical, social, or emotional manifestation.

Whether weak or strong, every being is worthy of the wish, "May they be at ease," because whether they're weak or strong, they're suffering. Ajahn Chah said, "Poor people suffer like poor people, rich people suffer like rich people; intelligent people suffer like intelligent people; and not-so-intelligent people suffer like not-so-intelligent people." That's the universal leveler: we all suffer.

I remember Ajahn Chah teasing us Westerners because we generally had far more education than most of the Thai monks who went to study, train, and ordain with him. As he became better-known, there were more Bangkok Thais coming who were well educated also. It was always a source of amusement to him. He would say, "You know, people go and study and they get bachelor's degrees, but their defilements get bachelor's degrees as well. Then they get master's degrees, and their defilements also get master's degrees. They say, well, this isn't satisfying, so they decide to get doctorates, but then their defilements get Ph.D.s as well."

It's the nature of beings immersed in greed, hatred, and delusion without liberating insight. We all suffer. Generating loving-kindness cuts across the board.

Another thing Ajahn Chah said—I can't resist—teasing us as Westerners because we came from an affluent society and had education: "Yeah, well, you Westerners have affluence and education. Look at the vultures—they fly really high but look at what they come down to eat." It was always a source of amusement to him.

The chant conveys the message of spreading loving-kindness to all living beings, "the seen and the unseen." Again, we realize that even if we don't see or know them on a personal level, we know that all beings are worthy and would respond to that wish to live in safety and happiness. "Living near or far away, those born and to be born." In the Pali, it's *sambhavesī vā*, those beings that are seeking birth: they don't know what they are in for. They think, "Boy, I can't wait to get born." They get bored with something, whatever realm they're in, and they think, "I want to be born, I want to be reborn." Of course, that's the cycle—it goes around and around.

So, having that deep sense of kindness and compassion towards all beings—*sabbe sattā sukhitā hontu,* "May all beings be at ease." *Sabbe sattā bhavantu sukhitattā,* "May all beings bring that happiness into being"—it then comes back to how we live with each other, living with loving-kindness.

"Let none deceive another": the commitment to real honesty and straightforwardness in our dealings with each other and, again, recognizing that how beings can have a sense of safety and happiness is by having a sense of trust with each other. "Let none deceive another." Be solidly committed to that which is true and try to be as upfront and clear with each other as possible.

It's also good to qualify that, bringing it back to the sense of being gentle in speech as well, because sometimes we can take truth as an ideal and forget the effect it's going to have on the ground. Skillfulness is very important in how we deal with each other.

"Or despise any being in any state": there is a common human tendency to lift oneself up by putting somebody else down. "Despise" is a very strong word, but it has the sense of looking down on somebody, blowing them off, or disregarding them in some way. As human beings we easily do that because there is a sense that criticizing or being able to put others down lifts ourselves up a bit. It's just not a very beautiful mental state.

When I went to Thailand, I had been traveling around the world for about a year and then was ordained as a Buddhist monk. After having been a monk for about sixteen years, I went back to Canada for the first time for a visit. After being in the rural culture of monasteries in the northeast of Thailand, which is quite a gentle culture, I found it quite painful to see how people spoke and talked, putting each other down. Being exposed to media and the sarcasm, critical put-downs, and snide comments: I found it very painful.

It's ordinary. I don't think my family was more egregious than anybody else. In fact, they were pretty good. It's just a norm within the culture. I think it's important to become very conscious of that, so that we aren't drawn into putting anybody down in any way, making fun of others, criticizing, or being sarcastic.

"Let none, through anger or ill will, wish harm upon another": this means protecting and sustaining your thoughts of loving-kindness and well-wishing, or at least neutrality. And then there is the phrase, "Even as a mother protects with her life her child, her only child." The Buddha very consciously uses the archetypal image of the mother who identifies with the child. It's her only child and therefore, there is a ceaseless well-wishing on her part. Even if a mother is not right there with the child, her antennae are out. The slightest sound pulls the mother back to check and make sure that the child is okay, so the image is very apt.

Then the Buddha says, "With a boundless heart should one cherish all living beings." The sense is that, in the way that the mother doesn't think of herself and her first thought is for the child, we, too, have that boundless quality through which we're not thinking of ourselves anymore, we're setting ourselves aside. We establish the quality of cherishing all living beings and radiating kindness, allowing those thoughts and feelings of kindness, of mettā, to permeate: "Spreading upwards to the skies and downward to the depths, outwards and unbounded, freed from hatred and ill will."

There is a sense of unobstructed radiating and of not choosing. Not saying, "I'll radiate upwards, downwards, out in all directions everywhere, except for that person." We don't have that limitation.

This emphasizes the quality of being freed from hatred and ill will and that the basis of loving-kindness is abiding in non-aversion. It's not being trapped by negativity, aversion, ill will, or irritation. It's important to recognize that though thoughts of irritation may come up in the mind, as long as we don't feed, nurture, or support them, they're just thoughts. Or if there is a memory or perception, as long as we don't invest in, believe in, or support it, then it doesn't have a landing place. It doesn't have a place to establish itself. So as long as we don't identify with it, it ceases.

The nature of the human mind is such that we have a whole bank of experiences, both internally, within ourselves, and externally, from society, that impinges on us. All of that can pop up in the mind as thoughts because that is what a mind is for, to provide thoughts. But as meditators, we have to use discernment. What are we going to invest in? What are we going to put our energy into?

That is where *kamma* is created, whether it be the mental *kamma* of investing in thoughts of ill will, aversion, and greed, or the mental *kamma* of investing in renunciation, loving-kindness, and compassion. We are making that choice. That's the *kamma* that we're creating.

Sometimes people think, perhaps if they're upset or devastated, "I had this terrible thought of aversion . . ." Well, did you act on it? No? Well, don't make a problem out of it.

Thoughts pop up in the same way that there are all kinds of things happening in the world around us. What do we pay attention to? Where do we allow our attention to rest and gather momentum? Abiding in loving-kindness is a conscious choice that we make, both for ourselves and on account of how it affects others.

"Whether standing or walking, seated or lying down." These are the four postures. If we're not doing one, we're doing another, 24/7. This is our opportunity for practice: whether sitting, walking, lying down, or standing.

"Free from drowsiness": of course, it helps not to let the mind get clouded. It isn't just any sort of drowsiness or sleepiness, however, but the kind of drowsiness or dopiness that can come from going on automatic pilot. We can drowse through all sorts of interactions and activities.

"One should sustain this recollection." The word that's used in the sutta itself is *sati*: to sustain this mindfulness, this awareness, this recollection. "This is a sublime abiding."

This is a chant that many of the people associated with monasteries know by heart. It's helpful to have these chants available so that when you chant, you can pick out phrases that resonate.

Things will resonate differently at different times. It's good to have a phrase or a whole series of phrases that help remind you.

During the time that I was on sabbatical in Thailand, a couple of years ago now, I was living on my own, and I used those phrases that I introduced yesterday a lot. Something that also struck a chord with me is the phrase, "Wishing in gladness and in safety, may all beings be at ease," in both English and Pali. Because I chant it in Pali all the time, the Pali is meaningful for me as well. So I would alternate back and forth. I would walk almsround and that would be the mantra. Not just repeating it as quickly as I could, but planting that seed and carrying it through, planting that seed and carrying it through, generating loving-kindness. I found it very fruitful.

So take some of these phrases and recollections and experiment with them. Work with them and see what happens.

Questions and Answers

Question: For me, there appears to be a fine line between paying attention to breath and controlling breath. Is it like with quantum physics: just being aware changes the phenomena?

Answer: That's absolutely true in the sense that, as we're attentive to the breath, in the same way as if we're really aware of a thought or an emotion, a change is already set in motion. It takes a degree of skill in crafting exactly how we are attentive. Sometimes we pay attention in a way in which we have a very fixed idea of what we want. We then of course set ourselves up to confirm that idea.

It's also true that we can pay attention to the breath with an idea that we would like to become peaceful, but there needs to be a certain letting go, a willingness not to have the "doer" get involved and try to make things be how we conceive of them. That sense of doing turns into busyness, tightness, and disappointment, or it turns into gratification: we get what we want, but then we realize that what we wanted doesn't fit in with what we would want if we could get it. We tie ourselves in knots that way.

So we need to direct attention to what is useful at this time. Is it useful to bring up a pleasing object? Is it useful to put forth a certain determination, digging our heels in and saying, "I've got to hold the line here"? Or is it recognizing, "I've really got to let go into spaciousness"?

So, there is attention, and the breath is the anchor that we can use to sustain and cultivate awareness and mindfulness. But once we get into controlling the breath or trying to control what we are getting out of it too much, we are going to feel tension, tightness, and frustration. There is a fine line and that comes through experience. Of course, suffering is a great teacher.

Q: What happens when someone carefully builds a fire, but it suddenly turns into a forest fire, uncontrollable, and the person experiences mania, delusions, and paranoia? What is the spiritual treatment for this?

A: One of the first spiritual treatments is to stop meditating. When there isn't a very solid anchor in what is real, when one is caught up in delusions, then it's important not to feed the desire to meditate or delight in those delusions, manic states, or paranoia.

That doesn't mean there is no spiritual treatment for such delusions because I think some of the most spiritual healing work that can be done is around keeping precepts, associating with people who are virtuous, and drawing close to teachings and good teachers. It's very grounding.

Also, there are all of the aspects of generosity, giving, and service. These are extremely positive qualities that nurture a sense of stability and feeling good about ourselves. Often, people go into manic states, delusions, and paranoia because they don't feel so good about themselves. They want to become something else and they do it through meditation. Then they push the mind to distance themselves from how they perceive themselves to be, trying to become something else. We so-called normal people also do that. We need to be attentive.

As a young monk and then as a young abbot, I thought meditation was a panacea, a remedy for everything. Experience has shown me that it's not. It is helpful to have pharmaceuticals around sometimes. When I was in Thailand, there was a stretch of quite a few years, my middle years as a monk when I first became the abbot of Wat Nanachat, when, at least once or twice a year, there would be somebody who would flip out.

Part of this is just being in a different culture. There is an actual type of psychosis that is generated by the disorientation of being in a different culture. Being in a different culture, in a monastery, and practicing . . . suffice it to say that in the early days of people getting interested in Buddhism in Asia, there were some pretty wild and wooly characters out there. A lot of them were my friends in the monastery.

In Thailand, a traditional society, when somebody in a monastery goes a bit off, the teacher would usually put them to work, get them into their bodies. They would work in the context of being surrounded by and connecting with people with good virtue and generosity. Don't send them off to meditate. Get them a shovel and get them working. It's really helpful.

Q: What is the definition of wholesome? The word connotes for me the '50s era of Ozzie and Harriet.

A: I think I mentioned earlier today that the Pali word is *kusala*: wholesome, skillful, beneficial. Intrinsic to a kusala state, or the *kusala-citta*, the mind that is happy and at ease, is well-being, *sukha*. There is a sense of peace and stability, and then there is a freedom from greed, hatred, and delusion, a certain purity or a lack of the stain of the different defilements. The opposite of this is *akusala*. With *akusala*, there is a sense of dukkha: dissatisfaction, suffering, disease in some way. With the *akusula-citta*, there is always a certain amount of restlessness or agitation, the inability to settle and be peaceful because of the presence of the fundamental roots of defilement. Greed, hatred, and delusion are its different manifestations. It's a helpful perspective to see that these are intrinsic to such states.

Q: If someone were to become a monastic at Abhayagiri, how would he go about doing so? What are the day-to-day activities of a monk? What are a monk's duties and responsibilities? How does this change from season to season and year to year? What do I need to know and consider before making such a commitment?

A: You have to know it's not fun. Generally, what would happen would be somebody would come to the monastery interested in practicing, training, and becoming a monastic, and he would stay a few months. He comes for an initial stay of a week, and then he comes back again and asks to stay longer. If he fits in with the community, he could be accepted to stay for a longer period of time.

He would be in the monastery for three or four months and then request the *anagārika* training, like Louis here, who is in white. He formally takes the eight precepts and makes a commitment for a year. He can leave at any time, but we encourage people to make that commitment. After someone has been there a few months, it's not that difficult to say, "Yes, I'd like to stay for a year." But we don't have people sign contracts or anything.

Then, as it's coming close to a year, assuming he wants to go further with training, he would request to take novice ordination, which is the ten precepts and brown robes. Sāmanera Kaccāna is a novice. It's the ten precepts, which are a little bit different. One does not handle money. That changes one's life. When someone goes into brown, we try to distance him from the kitchen more and also, no driving. Of course, Sāmanera Kaccāna couldn't drive anyway, for different reasons! Louis doesn't drive either, but again, for different reasons.

Similarly, in about a year, if somebody wants to go forward, then he could take the full monk's ordination and make a commitment to stay five years with the teacher. The decisions are community based, so he could be an anagārika or a novice longer, but it's approximately a year for each stage. This doesn't mean he would stay all of the time at the monastery because usually we'll send monks to study somewhere else for at least one year during that time. Like Tan Sampajāno: he is finishing his third year here and, at the end of this Rains Retreat period, he'll go to study in Thailand for a year.

As for day-to-day activities, as a general rule, we begin at 5 o'clock in the morning, with chanting and meditation. Then there is a short period of chores and then at 7 o'clock, a light breakfast, coffee, and tea. At 7:30 there is a community meeting during which we divide up the work for the day. We tend to keep the work period to just the morning. Some people could be going off to do some construction, while some people could be going up to work in the forest, trail work, office work, any number of the things involved in running a monastery.

Everyone comes back together at 11 o'clock for the main meal. We have our meal together, clean up, and then people can go back to their dwelling places, which are individual huts scattered through the forest. People practice on their own in the afternoon. Some may come down for tea at 5:30, some will stay up in the forest. Then we have the evening meeting at 7:30.

Right now, in the summertime, we're having our morning and evening meetings on the meditation platform in the forest. It doesn't have a roof, so once it starts to get too cold or wet, then we have meetings down below, where we have a small meeting hall.

Different monks will have different duties and responsibilities. The whole monastery is run by the resident community, so you have to take responsibility for looking after things, the day-to-day maintenance, cleaning, building new things. You learn some skills as well as learn how to sew your robes.

Sāmanera Kaccāna is getting ready for his monk's ordination, so he is deeply immersed in sewing his robes. His ordination is October 26, and his parents were here on the retreat. Unfortunately, his father was ill and had to leave. He recently had an operation and it wasn't working, so they had to leave. They were disappointed. They were the ones who introduced Sāmanera Kaccāna to Buddhism. Anybody can come to the monastery.

Q: How will I know I am experiencing loving-kindness?

A: Again, I think that it's important that we are attending to the experience of non-ill will, "not dwelling in aversion." That is a much more stable or steady indicator of the building of loving-kindness—ill will, aversion, and irritation are not overwhelming the mind. We aren't dwelling on it; we are able to let it go; we are able to recognize its bane.

Q: Please explain how to cultivate *muditā*. I've heard it described as "poor man's happiness."

A: Actually, the previous Upāsikā Day, the teaching day at the monastery last month, was billed as "The Other Brahmavihāras" because mettā tends to get all the press, and the other ones tend to be easily overlooked. *Muditā* is appreciative joy, sympathetic joy, delighting in the well-being or success of others. Its direct opposite, of course, is jealousy, comparing oneself to others and generating negative feelings on account of what others have. Within the human condition, it's fairly strong conditioning that we compare ourselves to others and then find ourselves coming up short.

It's not that easy to experience a sense of joy at the well-being, success, capabilities, and intelligence of others and not be intimidated by or in competition with others. Our conditioning is pretty strong, but if we are able to direct attention in that way and access that, then our chances of happiness are increased tremendously.

Generally, our happiness is dependent on our own success: getting what we want, experiencing something pleasurable that we like. So it's more focused around "me." In contrast, muditā encompasses everybody, and if our happiness is able to be generated by somebody else's goodness or delight—and there are another eight billion people on the planet—our chances go up tremendously. If you're a betting person, I would put my bets on that.

Q: What is the difference between *taṇhā* and *lobha*?

A: They are both forms of desire, Pali words for desire, but *lobha* is a bit more specific in terms of greed: covetousness, the desire that comes from greed. *Taṇhā* is a much more generic name for desire. In the very first discourse that the Buddha gave, he pointed to *taṇhā* as the cause of suffering and then he specified *kāma-taṇhā*, sensual desire, *bhava-taṇhā*, the desire for becoming, for being, that sense of the self trying to establish itself, and *vibhava-taṇhā*, the desire for non-being, non-becoming, which is pushing away, rejection, fear, aversion.

So *taṇhā* is a much broader term for desire, and it can manifest in aversion, ill will, fear, as well as sensual desire. *Lobha* is much more a sense of greed and is not necessarily focused on say, the sensual, but is an underlying desire seeking an object that is gratifying.

Q: "Non-contention" is a highfalutin word. What does it mean?

A: We are always trying to find language to encapsulate something. Contention is based in aversion, a sense of competition, and is generated through a sense of dislike. There is a certain ill will there. When somebody is contentious, it's usually fraught with aversion or irritation. So non-contention is where we aren't approaching the world, other people, or our internal mental states from a base of aversion, fear, or manipulation. It's more an attitude of: "This is the way it is. I don't have to contend with it. I don't have to manipulate it. I don't have to force it to be anything else. It can just be what it is." That is the underlying quality of non-contention. We can just let things be as they are, which isn't so easy.

Q: Would you talk more about working with the hindrance of doubt?

A: One of the things with doubt is recognizing the tendency to uncertainty and wavering that comes when there is doubt in the mind. There is uncertainty, wavering, not being sure. Then how do we fill that gap? We tend either to fill it with projections of fear and aversion or with some distraction, such as eating: "Just give me something to eat, so I don't have to deal with this doubt."

This is when mindfulness of the body is really helpful. Tuning in to and recognizing the actual feeling, that vibration of doubt and uncertainty that comes into the mind and body and then impels us towards some way of covering up that doubt. Doubt is a miserable state to be with, so we want to ameliorate it in some way.

Recognizing and being able to relax around the doubt: this is when the body is really helpful. We can start to relax around that doubt and uncertainty, release the tightness and tension that is impelling us to move into something just to get out of the doubt. Start to tune in to: "How does it make my heart, mind, and body feel? What do I actually feel when there's doubt?"

There is that sense of wavering and uncertainty, when we hold back. To be able to step into it and not be paralyzed or overwhelmed—not reacting blindly—enables us to get out of that feeling of doubt and uncertainty. So these are some skillful ways of working with doubt. What needs to be recognized and brought out into the light of awareness is: "This is doubt."

One of the images that the Buddha gives for the hindrance of doubt is a dish of muddy water that is then placed in a dark cupboard (A 5.193). The murky quality of the water is not seen, not clearly understood, and not recognized, so it is put in the cupboard and hidden away. The first thing we need to do is to bring it out into the light of awareness and say: "This is doubt; this is unclear to me. I'm uncertain about this. I don't know."

It's interesting to pay attention to how many times in a conversation, when somebody asks you something and you give an answer, you respond not because you actually know the answer, but because you don't want anybody else to recognize that you don't know. You try to prop up the illusion of certainty. So, when somebody asks you something, it's a huge breakthrough to have the confidence to say, "I don't really know," rather than think, "I'd better say something quickly or they're going to think that I'm dumb." Just say, "Well, I don't know." It's actually quite easy, but it's amazing to watch the mind over and over again propping up the illusion of certainty, when in truth you're doubtful about what something is. These are some perspectives on doubt.

Q: I have an ongoing problem with certain vibrations. Here the most problematic is the recording device. The trunk of my body feels like it is vibrating as it moves into the room, just like the hum of the machine. When I get some concentration and I can see the fear, doubt, and thoughts that arise, I sometimes meet them skillfully; at other times, I lose skillful means. Any suggestions would most gratefully be received.

A: One approach would be tuning in to the body itself, recognizing that we can influence the feelings around us, particularly internally, if something is agitating. We can pay attention to something like the breath or the feeling somewhere in the body—picking a spot that feels comfortable, bringing our attention to a place that feels at ease.

It's easy for the mind to home in on something that we are irritated by or feel uncomfortable with. That is what grabs attention. But the conscious directing of attention to something that is more soothing and comfortable is a necessary part of living a human life because we are constantly surrounded by things that we like or dislike, that are pleasant or unpleasant, that are agreeable or disagreeable.

If the mind drifts into and homes into the disagreeable, the unpleasant, the things that we dislike, then we keep spinning around that. Certainly the definition of loving-kindness that I've used on several occasions, dwelling in non-aversion, is really a helpful tool. The mettā practice, that dwelling in non-aversion, is a helpful base because of the nature of the world.

One of the classic structures or aspects of the teaching is the worldly *dhammas*: praise and blame, honor and disrepute, happiness and suffering, and gain and loss. These are basic things that are going on all the time. It's easy to be drawn into or be fearful of say, criticism: to be elated when we get a bit of praise and to try to manipulate conditions so that there is more praise and less criticism, more gain and less loss. It's natural, but it's also energy intensive. Sometimes it works, and sometimes it doesn't.

It's much more helpful, from a perspective of practice, to see that there is that which is pleasant and unpleasant, success and failure, whether it is material, worldly, or in spiritual practice. Allow that to take place and allow it to be there without being drawn into the things that generate the unskillful tendencies or that tend to create more agitation and suffering in the mind.

As a young monk watching Ajahn Chah, it was tremendously inspiring. It was as if he was this peaceful, happy presence in the center of the universe. Things happened around him all the time. People praised him, people criticized him, many people were drawn to him. Monks would ordain out of inspiration, monks would leave out of frustration and disillusionment, and Ajahn Chah was always happy, regardless.

You realize that that is really possible in the human condition. You don't need to have conditions that are always perfect. Ajahn Chah really didn't have a life of his own. He was just there for people. He wasn't looking to have anything special for himself. The nature of the world is such that there are always things that jar or grate as well as things that are pleasant. We obviously don't go around trying to find the things that are jarring and grating just to test ourselves or make ourselves strong. We have enough of that in ordinary circumstances. So it's more of how to work with letting go, with loving-kindness. These are the tools.

Q: Would you be willing to repeat the mettā phrases that you taught us yesterday and today? The only one I can remember is, "May I be prosperous."

A: Those filters are working all the time. One is, "May I be well, happy, peaceful, and prosperous. May no harm come to me. May no difficulties come to me. May no problems come to me. May I always meet with spiritual success. May I have the patience, courage, understanding, and determination to meet and overcome inevitable difficulties, problems, and failures in life."

These are the phrases. It's helpful to get these fully embedded in memory, so you're not thinking, "What the heck was that phrase that he was saying?" Committing it to memory turns it into a kind of mantra that you can use. This is what is called *parikamma* in Pali, a repetition that is useful for establishing concentration or consistent mindfulness. These mettā phrases are skillful tools for setting a tone within the mind.

Skillful Thinking in Meditation

*Directing thought to loving-kindness is a skillful way
of using and applying the mind that allows us to
build a momentum of wholesomeness.*

In meditation, when we are trying to calm and still the mind, I think it's a common tendency to try to eliminate thinking and get rid of the thinking mind. A common equation comes up: "I think, therefore I suffer. If I didn't think, I wouldn't suffer. Buddhism is for the overcoming of suffering, so I must annihilate thinking."

Usually what happens then is either the thinking explodes or we tie ourselves into knots trying not to think. We might be quite successful in pushing down and suppressing thought, but it never feels very good.

Directing thought to loving-kindness is a skillful way of using and applying thought in a way that allows the mind to build a momentum of skillfulness and wholesomeness. The thoughts are increasingly on the side of that which is kusala. The very nature of the kusala-citta is that it's peaceful, settled, and has a steady quality to it.

Another useful way of directing thought is to the aspects of what in Pali is called *saṃvega*: urgency, the sense that there is no time to waste or to fool around. One of the reflections that the monastics are encouraged to cultivate on a regular basis is: "The days and nights are relentlessly passing. How well am I spending my time?" That's a very useful reflection because it is real: days and nights are relentlessly passing. They don't pass benignly. Each day that passes, we're older and that much closer to death. That's the reality: I managed to make it through another day, but I still have death as a reality that I am going to have to face.

So that is the sense of urgency. Letting time slip by in a way that's frivolous, empty, or just propping up old habit patterns, recycling our trusty companions of greed, hatred, and delusion: where does that get us? We've all done it. We've all seen that it's not so fruitful.

Bringing up those motivations for urgency—aging, sickness, and death; the impermanence and uncertainty of the mind and its moods—is a skillful antidote to complacency. It's not something to flog ourselves with and turn into a neurotic obsession, but it's something that is essential in terms of needing to prod ourselves and not waste opportunities.

Urgency is not a frantic quality in the mind. A sense of urgency is a sense of motivation: "Yes, I want to get up and get moving, get up and have the opportunity to use the time skillfully, to develop virtue, to train in that which is peaceful and to establish myself in wisdom and discernment." These are motivations. Again, it's not to turn urgency into something that has a frantic or a manic edge to it; that isn't particularly useful. But it is helpful to have a sense of urgency.

Saṃvega is a very positive mental state and motivation. As we use directed thought, it's helpful in meditation or in ordinary circumstances to be able to review the five hindrances. These particular tendencies of the mind are the fundamental qualities that bring us to a place of non-peacefulness and lack of clarity.

So, to review the five hindrances: sensual desire, ill will, sloth and torpor, restlessness and worry, and doubt. In terms of directed thought, see if they're present, how to work with them, and how they arise.

If there is sensual desire, what are we directing thought towards? We're usually directing thought towards something we perceive as pleasurable, delightful, and capable of gratification. So that directed thought is then grabbed by the hindrances and defilements and ends up agitating the mind.

When thought is directed towards ill will, aversion, irritation, anger, and displeasure, then it feeds the hindrance. That feeding of the hindrance makes it healthy and strong. We don't want healthy and strong hindrances; we would be better off starving them. Don't feed them.

I remember Ajahn Chah saying one time, "You've got a cat that comes around—*meow, meow, meow*—and you think, 'This poor cat!' And you feed it. Sure enough, it's back again, on the porch every morning." At Abhayagiri, people wonder why we don't have any dogs or cats. If you feed them, they just keep coming around, and they usually tell their friends as well.

If what we are doing with our hindrances is feeding them, we end up with multiple hindrance attacks. Pay attention instead to: "If I don't feed it, if I don't direct thought towards the stimulus of the hindrance, then it fades." That opens up a space, and we can direct attention positively. Especially with ill will, the positive directing of thought towards mettā is a very skillful application of directed thought.

Sloth and torpor happen when we direct thought towards fullness after the meal. We feel a certain lassitude and disinterest. That feeds sloth and torpor. So, just as a training, don't let the mind rest on things that would tend towards sloth and torpor, to dullness. If we pay attention to it, then the mind absorbs into it, so that lassitude or dullness starts to take over. Withdraw attention and thought from those areas of the mind that are obscure, dull, and amorphous. Especially in meditation, different mental states drift in and drift out of the mind. If we let the mind dwell on the more obscure, amorphous, and drifty states of mind, that's where we end up, with a mind that's very dull. So it's important to direct attention and feed the ability of the mind to focus and center on something that is brightening, sharpening, and clarifying.

How we direct our attention and thought is the same with restlessness and doubt. So, the five hindrances are a very useful area of reflection in terms of how best to bring up and establish attention. Because when we do direct attention in a way that is not dissipated through the distraction of the five hindrances, then the mind actually becomes very steady and strong.

There is a strength there. The Buddha compares it to a mountain stream (A 5:51). If the stream comes down from the mountain and is then channeled off into different little canals and rivulets, the power of the stream is dissipated. It's not able to wash anything away. That is compared to the energy and flow of the mind as it's dissipated out into the five hindrances. When it goes off into these different hindrances, the strength of that current or stream is just not so strong. Of course, the opposite is true. When a stream comes down and is not dissipated, it has tremendous power and can be used for something beneficial.

At Abhayagiri, we're trying to set up a micro-hydro system. If the stream goes off in all sorts of different directions, all you get is a piddly little amount. The turbine goes *kerchunk, kerchunk*, and you get no power or electricity. Whereas if you can get that channel going in one direction, you can generate a lot of electricity and you don't have to pay the electricity company.

This is natural. These are attributes of nature. It's just the mind. But it's important to be attentive and recognize how these patterns and tendencies work.

Then, what happens when we direct thought in a particular way towards the hindrances? What is the result when we're able to ameliorate and set aside the five hindrances and allow the attention to settle and focus? Since the theme of this retreat is mettā, as the five hindrances go into abeyance, we can bring more attention to the mettā-nimitta and allow that to shine forth. We can then direct thought in a way that supports the feeling of well-wishing, softness within the heart, and brightness that holds oneself and others dear. Allow thought to be directed to the feeling of loving-kindness.

Thoughts are there to help as reminders. Underlying them is the particular feeling of spaciousness and warmth in the mind and heart. Allow that to establish itself through the body, directing it toward yourself. The mind is able to keep guarding the sustained application of the thoughts or feelings of loving-kindness.

The Pali words are *vitakka* and *vicāra*. *Vitakka* is what is translated as thought or directed thought, but it's both the thought and the bringing of the thought, feeling, or perception up into the mind. That's all vitakka. The arising of the thought of loving-kindness and directing of attention to loving-kindness, whether on the level of thought, feeling, or perception, are all vitakka. *Vicāra* is the sustaining or continuing of that. But there is also an evaluation that goes on: "How am I holding it? How is it sustaining itself? What does it feel like? What's its texture?"

There is the initial bringing up of attention into the mind. Then there is the sustaining of that. There is an evaluation, but it's not an intellectual evaluation. It's getting a feeling for the texture of that thought and the feeling within the mind so that it's sustained and we are able to look at it in a different way.

Vitakka is bringing that up into view within the mind, in the same way that I've just lifted up the bell-striker. Vicāra is looking at it from different angles. There is an interest there able to sustain it. We get distracted. Okay then, vitakka, bring it up again.

That's what we are doing with the thoughts of loving-kindness or the meditation object at any time. We are using that process of directed thought and evaluation so that there is a gaining of momentum of interest and attention towards that object. With the object of loving-kindness, it's that feeling.

It's not going to be homogeneous or consistent. But that is how we use vitakka and vicāra. We are not trying to make it absolutely consistent. Directed thought and evaluation recognize those different textures and maintain the basic theme of loving-kindness.

Of course, the same is true in terms of whatever meditation object we are using, say the breath. That is what makes the breath interesting. We can determine to make this breath interesting just by focusing. It's through looking at it, lifting it up, and viewing it from different angles that we can do that. Then the mind is able to settle a bit longer and stay steadily on it.

Then part of the evaluation is recognizing that this is starting to feel good: "My body is feeling more comfortable and settled." So, there is a recognition of the effect.

With loving-kindness as a meditation object, we encourage ourselves with saṃvega. We are attentive to the five hindrances, and then we direct thought and evaluation to the object of loving-kindness.

One of the very powerful aspects of loving-kindness is that, as loving-kindness gets stronger, the tendency towards ill will and aversion drops. It can't land in the mind so easily. There is a very strong positive force that also then helps ameliorate the other hindrances that are akusala. It's a really good bridge towards the steadiness of mind that we are cultivating in conjunction with mindfulness of breathing and awareness of the body. Loving-kindness allows the mind to make the bridge between the point where the hindrances are still kicking in a bit and a place where it is more exclusively wholesome and settled. Wholesome and bright mental states rely on loving-kindness.

The sense of seclusion from sensual desire and unwholesome mental states creates a very real shift through which the mind can then settle into its object. Whether that object is the mettā-nimitta or the breath depends on what we are comfortable with. But mettā provides a very stable bridge into that steadiness of mind where the mind is able to unify. Unification of the mind is disrupted by those little rivulets going off in different directions: to sensual desire, ill will, sloth and torpor, restlessness, or doubt.

Allow the mind to bridge that gap and develop interest in something that is more positive. It's quite natural. As human beings, we are hardwired to prefer pleasure to pain. So if we can see something that is really pleasurable, then the mind can unify with that.

Something as pleasurable as the feeling of loving-kindness is able to bridge across the habit patterns of restlessness, doubt, or drifting, and go to that steadiness of mind.

As we practice and work with vitakka and vicāra by bringing up and sustaining positive thought, something pleasurable, bright, and joyful arises in the mind. We are not doing anything wrong. It's all right to feel that. You may get excited and start to analyze. Instead, give yourself permission to enjoy meditation.

As human beings, we haplessly bumble into old patterns: "Here I am, back suffering again. At least it's familiar and feels secure." Rather, allow the mind to explore the regions of well-being and happiness. Confidence can be there, because it's not just pleasure arising out of trying to get something gratifying in terms of a sensual hit. It's more deeply satisfying and joyful when based on purity of intention and an unalloyed quality of skillfulness. It's wholesome.

In the story of the Buddha, when he was still the Bodhisattva and striving for awakening, he struggled with ascetic practices. He got to the point where he was emaciated and frustrated. He then had a memory of when he was a young child: becoming very peaceful, settled, and concentrated when he was left on his own during a ceremony. He was about nine years old and his mind went into stillness. He recalled that memory and wondered, "Why am I afraid of that happiness that is untainted by sensuality and unskillful tendencies? Perhaps that's the path." There was a realization that there is actually nothing wrong with that kind of happiness. Then the Buddha thought that he would never be able to cultivate that path in his emaciated shape, so he started eating again. That is when he had the insight into the Middle Way (M 4).

So, cultivation relies on directed thought and uses the investigative process, the ability to pay attention and allow the mind to channel its energies. Not attending to things that are disruptive to the mind, but being able to sustain attention on those things that are nurturing to the mind and heart: that is how the mind is able to unify. It doesn't happen by chance or just by sitting long enough, as if you're going to get peaceful if you put in enough hours.

In my early years as a monk, I remember another monk in my monastery. He had been ordained for several years, but he never appeared very peaceful to me. As I got to know him, I found that from the time he first started meditating, he had a journal and kept track of every meditation session he'd ever had and how many hours and minutes he'd meditated. It was kind of like, "If I build my account up enough, somehow, I'm going to get peaceful."

Well, no. You have to be doing it in the right way. You actually have to be skillful. So learn those skills of directing attention: What do you feed? What do you starve? What do you pay attention to? What do you ignore? What do you encourage? What do you discourage? It takes some discernment and reflection.

Then recognize that there are intrinsic effects of different mental states, such as anger, ill will, and restlessness. They have an intrinsic effect on the mind; they are agitating. Loving-kindness, the quality of compassion, respect for truth: these are all things that have a deeply settling effect within the heart.

So allow the mind to attend to that. Allow the mind to sustain that attention. And then realize how the mind can unify, relying on that. Sometimes there are overtones of interpretation or meaning that come from particular words. When we talk about concentration, just the word concentration tends to have a feeling of "me, concentrating, forcing my mind on something and holding it there." But that doesn't really convey what we actually do. Unification, on the other hand, involves directed thought, evaluation, joy, and well-being. The mind can be unified in the sense that it's unified in this feeling of well-being and peace, of being very settled and steady. It's all working together and comes together in a place of steadiness. So these are some reflections this morning for meditation.

Guided Mettā Meditation

As we are able to establish the wish for well-being,
this loving-kindness lays the foundation for the
qualities of compassion, sympathetic joy,
and equanimity.

As we cultivate this meditation on loving-kindness, a variety of formulations can be used. Some of them can be quite complicated and some quite simple. What is most important is to recognize how it works, how it affects us. What is it that resonates and helps bring into being a feeling and perception of loving-kindness, an interest in the wish for well-being in oneself and others?

As a meditation, the use of words and phrases is a helpful way of establishing mindfulness or recollections. We can use a phrase to plant that seed within the heart and mind. Because the nature of the mind is to come up with different thoughts and, usually, with stories (not just short, little sentences here or there), we use those phrases to help keep the mind on track: "Oh right, I'm doing loving-kindness meditation."

So using those phrases, perhaps from the Buddha's discourse on loving-kindness—"Wishing in gladness and in safety, may all beings be at ease" or "May I be well, happy, and peaceful"—is a way of keeping the mind on track and reminding it what it's intending to do. So that is actually the meditation; that is how we train the mind.

In Thailand, one of the most common meditation methods or techniques is using the word "*buddho*," the name of the Buddha.

"*bud-*" on the in-breath and "*-dho*" on the out breath: just that simple word. If you want, you can use the word "mettā": "met-" on the in-breath and "-tā" on the out-breath. Use that word to keep the mind on track. Tune in to the feeling, the connotations of mettā you have reflected on. This helps the mind to channel its attention and energy to the pleasing emotional tone of well-wishing.

In meditation practice, mettā has the very useful function of providing emotional moisture. If you think, "*Anicca, dukkha, anattā, anicca, dukkha, anattā, anicca, dukkha, anattā,*" it gets pretty dry after a while. "Impermanence, unsatisfactoriness, not-self, impermanence, unsatisfactoriness, not-self" are very true. However, the mind has to be prepared and balanced. Mettā-bhāvanā can be a very useful basis for providing a sense of moisture, warmth, and brightness to the mind.

The opposite is true as well. If you really see impermanence, unsatisfactoriness, and not-self, one of the sure indications that the insight is a true one is the sense of universal kindness and well-wishing that arises. You think, "Wow, everyone is in the same boat." Then there is a sense of caring, the heart's natural response to a deep insight.

Usually, we don't start with deep insights. It's good to sprinkle in a bit of mettā to lubricate the insights and heart so that it's ready, ripe, and able to respond. Also, as we continue in this particular spiritual practice, it is quite natural to become inured or accustomed to the particular pattern of reflection, investigation, and practice we are doing. So having supportive practices helps create a broad base for practice and insight to ripen. It gives us the energy for practice.

Today I'd like to introduce as a meditation, the chant, "Reflections on Universal Well-Being," which are all four brahmavihāras. Almost half of the chant is specifically about mettā, loving-kindness. I think that is quite appropriate in that mettā is really the doorway into the other brahmavihāras. As we are able to establish the wish for well-being, this loving-kindness lays the foundation for the qualities of compassion, sympathetic joy, and equanimity. To try to establish equanimity or sympathetic joy on its own is not that easy, but loving-kindness is an appropriate doorway into these sublime abidings.

The chant begins with a very direct statement: in Pali, *aham̐ sukhito homi*, which is "May I be happy." Of course, if you're chanting "May I be happy," it falls a bit flat. Whereas, if you begin a chant, "May I abide in well-being," it's kind of nice to chant.

"May I be happy" is a very precise translation of *aham̐ sukhito homi*, but I think it is appropriate to take a bit of poetic license, to make it a bit more chantable: "May I abide in well-being." For me, having chanted this for decades now, that is what happens when I think of the words. When I use it as a meditation, it comes out as a chant. It's kind of hard for me just to say it.

It's a very beautiful chant. Establish that wish: "May I abide in well-being, may I abide in happiness, may I abide in the basis of all that is pleasurable and delightful." The wish directs attention to oneself. That is very much the classical mode of the cultivation of loving-kindness: to direct attention inward and establish that very strong feeling of well-wishing towards oneself.

In the scriptures, there is a very lovely exchange between King Pasenadi and Queen Mallikā. He was the king of Kosala, in which is Sāvatthi, where the Buddha spent the majority of his Rains residences in Jeta's Grove and elsewhere in the region. So he was very familiar with King Pasenadi. Queen Mallikā was a devout Buddhist and had a solid practice. King Pasenadi had tremendous faith in the Buddha, but there is never any mention of him having attained any levels of liberation.

In any event, in the palace, King Pasenadi asks Queen Mallikā, "Who is it that you cherish the most?" Queen Mallikā replies, "Well, I cherish myself the most." "Hmmm," he thinks. He always takes her lead. He has tremendous love and respect for her, so there must be something to this.

Pasenadi goes to the Buddha and recounts the conversation. The Buddha says, "That's exactly what one's attitude should be and that's how it is in reality. It's when we cherish and honor ourselves fully that we can really look after and cherish others. We need to have that foundation." (S 3.8) It isn't a selfish obsession with "me." In reality, we do need to cherish ourselves.

If I eat something, nobody else gets full. We relate to ourselves first on a cellular level. So, on an emotional level, we need to attend to ourselves in appropriate and skillful ways. When we look after ourselves, attend to our well-being, that is when we can be a refuge and be there for others. As human beings, we're not all that different, despite all of our assumptions about our fascinating uniqueness. We're not very different, so when we tune in and understand ourselves, we can be really present for others. It's our unskillful obsession with ourselves that blocks us off from others.

So, establish that sense of "May I abide in well-being." Take that in and open the heart to the sincere wish, "May I abide in well-being and freedom from affliction." In Pali the phrase is *niddukkho homi*, without dukkha, without suffering. *Avero homi* is "In freedom from hostility." *Vera* is conflict and also grudges—the grudges and conflicts that ironically bind us together. In Thai, there is a phrase that you say when something goes wrong. In English, we say, "Oh, shoot." In Thai, it's "*wain gam*," "Oh, this is conflict and kamma." Establish the wish, "May I abide in freedom from hostility," in freedom from any kind of conflict.

"*Abyāpajjho homi*": freedom from ill will. *Byāpāda* is ill will, anger, irritation, aversion. "May I abide in freedom from ill will." *Anīgho homi*: in freedom from anxiety, worry, or fear. Establish that wish, "May I abide in freedom from anxiety."

Sukhī attānaṃ pariharāmi: *attā* is me, self. "May I be happy, and may I maintain well-being in myself." Draw attention to that wish for freedom from affliction, hostility, ill will, and anxiety, and that wish to maintain well-being. Establish yourself as grounded in well-being. As you develop this as a meditation, going through the phrases, you can repeat it many times until it feels solid and you feel grounded in well-being.

Then allow it to be a bit more non-directional: not directed toward yourself, but a bit more pervasive: "May everyone abide in well-being." In the Pali, *sabbe sattā sukhitā hontu*: "May all beings abide in well-being; may all beings be happy." Then proceed to similar recollections or aspirations. *Sabbe sattā averā hontu*: "May all beings abide in freedom from hostility, ill will, and anxiety." Those feelings of fear, worry, and anxiety are part of not just the human condition, but the universal condition of having a life force, whether it's a human being, a mammal, or an insect. As soon as you have a life force, you're protecting it. Every being wants to get away from pain or any kind of threat.

Of course, there is going to be some kind of threat. Living in the forest, animals are constantly attuned to danger. Abhayagiri is in the forest, and there are lots of animals there. Deer, particularly the does, don't have any clear physical means of aggression, but they have big ears and they are listening. They have big eyes and they're on the lookout for anything that might be a bit threatening. There is anxiety there. That is the nature of being born into a physical body: we are vulnerable. We can obsess on this and keep spinning ourselves out with anxiety.

There is a book by Robert Sapolsky, *Why Zebras Don't Get Ulcers*. If there is danger and a lion attacks, zebras are out of there as quickly as they can. They might even be mauled or see a friend mauled, but as soon as it's over, they're out there grazing again. Human beings, on the other hand, are constantly planning about the next perceived threat, which may or may not happen. And we end up with ulcers. It's a response that serves us well in certain circumstances, but when it's applied across the board, it doesn't really serve us that well. Dwelling in anxiety is exceedingly uncomfortable.

On the sheet of paper I passed out on the sharing of loving-kindness, there is a very similar formulation, with a bit of a twist that is very nice. But it uses those same structures and is very classical. It is out of a very early commentarial treatise, the *Paṭisambhidāmagga*, which is so old it's in the Pali Canon. These are the formulations for one of the ways for the cultivating of loving-kindness: developing freedom from hostility, freedom from ill will, freedom from anxiety, and then the wish for happiness. So that as we cultivate this recitation and recollection, we cultivate the feeling, "May I be well, happy, and peaceful. And just as I wish to be well, happy, and peaceful, may all beings be well, happy, and peaceful."

This is recognizing that that wish is not just isolated or focused solely on oneself. "In the same way that I wish to be well, happy, and peaceful, may all beings experience that. May I be free from animosity. As I wish to be free from animosity, may all beings be free from animosity. May I be free from any kind of suffering. And as I wish to be free from any kind of suffering, may all beings be free from any kind of suffering. May I live in peace and happiness. And as I wish to live in peace and happiness, may all beings live in peace and happiness."

These are helpful phrases or structures. It's helpful to become knowledgeable about Pali, the scriptural language, because sometimes our own English language has a backlog of associations and habit patterns that affect our thoughts and condition our reactions. As we delve into Buddhism, the Pali language, and not just these phrases, can be very helpful.

The only function the Pali language has performed over the last 2,300 years or so is to maintain the discourses of the Buddha. It's a technical language, and the Buddha probably spoke something very similar—there's controversy about that. Pali is a mid-Indian, ancient dialect in which the scriptures were written. So even if it wasn't exactly what the Buddha spoke at that time, it's very, very close. And its only function has been to pass on the words of the Buddha, the scriptures, and the teachings. It's a technical language geared to spiritual themes.

As I've been mentioning over the past couple of days, "kusala" and "akusala" are technical terms that point to a particular state of mind that is wholesome, skillful, and beneficial and the opposite, respectively. They have particular parameters. Taṇhā is a specific desire rooted in greed, hatred, delusion, and non-recognition of the way things truly are. When the Buddha says taṇhā is the source of suffering, he's not saying desire, as a generic term, is the source of suffering. Rather, it's a specific form of desire. So, it's helpful sometimes, as an exercise, to familiarize yourself with some of the basic terms. Then things start to leap out.

As you consciously cultivate the quality of loving-kindness, bring attention to "May I abide in well-being," trying to establish that wish firmly and clearly towards yourself within the heart. But it doesn't just affect you; it transforms you and, by transforming you, it has an effect on the world and people around you. After a week of loving-kindness practice and training, go back home or to your workplace and take note of anything you find different there. Or does someone say in disbelief, "You've come back from a week of loving-kindness?"

There is a story in the *Visuddhimagga*, a commentarial treatise, about a man from India who hears about Sri Lanka and how there are lots of people practicing meditation there. This is almost 1,000 years after the Buddha passed away. Big changes happened in India at that time, and Buddhism was flourishing in Sri Lanka. He has the intention to take ordination, so he gives up his business, takes leave of his family, travels to Sri Lanka, and takes ordination. He is interested in loving-kindness meditation, so he gets instruction and goes to live in a place where many meditators are practicing loving-kindness meditation.

He lives in a particular hut in the forest, surrounded by a nice grove of trees. He is very assiduous in his cultivation of loving-kindness meditation and practices diligently for four or five months. Then a wish comes into his mind, "Maybe I'll go off to another monastery and practice with such and such a teacher."

With the formulation of that wish, he hears sobbing outside his dwelling place. So, he goes out and there is this deity who lives in a big tree nearby. He asks what is wrong, and the deity says, "You just had the thought that you want to leave, and it makes me sad. While you've been here practicing loving-kindness, I've been happy and all of the beings around here have been happy. If you leave, all the other devas and non-human beings are going to go back to arguing and quarreling, just like they used to do. While you've been here practicing, everything has been peaceful."

So he stays longer and continues with his practice. In good Buddhist fashion, this happens three times. Finally, he gives up his determination to go anywhere and stays there and attains enlightenment, which is what always seems to happen in the stories.

One could say it's just a shaggy dog story from the scriptures, but I know of a monk who had something very similar happen. He really embodies loving-kindness. He's still living—his name is Ajahn Gunha, and he is a nephew of Ajahn Chah. Now, he's well into his sixties. He had some major realizations when he was a junior monk. When he was a younger monk, he practiced diligently, and the quality of loving-kindness is a predominant feature of his being.

He was traveling by himself one time, before he established a regular monastery. This was along the border of Burma, in an area where there were big expanses of jungle but also a lot of insurgents. He was walking through the jungle when he walked into a large encampment of Communist insurgents. They immediately surrounded him with weapons and tried to grill him: "How did he get in there?" They thought he was a government spy because the whole area around their encampment was mined and he had been able to walk through the minefields. They held him for a long time and continued to question him. But eventually, when they realized he had been telling the truth and had indeed walked through their minefields without having been blown up, they warmed up to him and looked after him and fed him.

After some time, they were convinced that he was a genuine monk and that they should let him go. They accompanied him, seeing him out through the minefields, and set him on his way. Then they came back and there was a realization: "Why did we let him go? It was so nice having a monk here. Everybody was living harmoniously and happily. He was such a wonderful presence for us." So they tromped out after him and invited him to come back. They would look after him for the Rains Retreat. He had already made a commitment to spend the Rains in another place but expressed appreciation for their offer. So, that is that presence of loving-kindness. "While he was here, everything felt good."

So, let's take some time just to sit and use these phrases, this particular structure. Establish ease, alertness, and comfort in the posture. Allow the breathing to be natural, easeful. Relax any kind of tension. Allow the breath to come in very, very clearly, without any obstruction. Allow the breath to go out without any obstruction, not controlling, just feeling very comfortable and at ease.

As you physically feel at ease, attention and mindfulness are present. Then formulate the wish, "May I abide in well-being." Allow the breath to come in and go out. Allow the heart to resonate around that sincere wish, "May I abide in well-being. May I abide in happiness. May I abide in freedom from affliction." Allow that to resonate through the body and the mind. "May I abide in freedom from suffering and discomfort—mental, physical, any kind of dukkha." Establish that wish toward yourself, cherishing yourself with the sincere wish for freedom from anything that is afflicting, obstructing.

Allow that wish to be an energy within the body and mind. Allow that energy to flow through and permeate the whole body, the whole mind: that sincere wish for happiness, freedom from suffering.

"May I abide in freedom from hostility." Allow the mind to relinquish and release any kind of hostile, aversive, or negative intention toward yourself or others because the first person harmed when you formulate an intention of hostility or aversion is you. Release and relinquish any negativity with the clear intention or wish: "May I abide in freedom from hostility. May I abide in freedom from ill will." Again, not setting up any kind of contention or conflict, put it all down and direct that wish, feeling, and aspiration for well-being toward yourself.

"May I abide in freedom from anxiety." Recognize the inevitable tendency toward fear, worry, and anxious wondering, but set the intention: "May I abide in freedom from any kind of anxiety." Recognize that it would be a very different world for you and others around you if there was freedom from such anxiety and fear.

"May I maintain well-being in myself." Return to the wish, the aspiration for stability of well-being, a steady sense of happiness that comes when the mind is not overwhelmed by negative habits of mind. Recognize that this is actually possible. It's a noble aspiration to set for yourself. It's holding yourself dear, cherishing yourself in an appropriate way.

Allow these aspirations and recollections, this loving-kindness, to permeate and pervade the body and mind. As that is increasingly well-established and feels stable, allow the focus to be broader. Expand the focus so that it encompasses everything around you, inclusive of all others. "May all beings abide in well-being. May everyone abide in well-being. May everyone abide in freedom from hostility."

We can't force the world and all beings to live that way, but we can have that aspiration. We can perceive the benefit. Hold that within the heart. "May everyone abide in freedom from ill will." We can see the suffering and pain that arise from ill will, so develop that sincere wish of compassion, friendliness, and care. Wish that all beings abide in freedom from ill will.

Allow the heart to be open and expansive, wishing safety and security. "May everyone abide in freedom from anxiety."

"May all beings maintain well-being in themselves." As we're able to establish that intention without division within the mind, we stop separating anybody out into "us" and "them," my group and that group. Develop that expansive wish and aspiration, that everyone be able to maintain well-being in him or herself. This allows the mind to break down the barriers of how we habitually compare and divide, and suffer because of it.

Cultivation of these phrases and tuning in to the feelings they generate are helpful for the cultivation of a mood of loving-kindness, and they also give us an insight into the way the mind works: how we cherish or overlook ourselves, how we look at others, how we compare, how we judge. In the loving-kindness meditation, when we allow the heart to abide in kindness and well-being there is no judging or comparing.

Questions and Answers

So, we'll begin this evening's question period. Nature abhors a vacuum and we managed to get through all the submitted questions last night. The basket is full again, which is a good sign.

Question: One of my lay insight meditation teachers said, "The Western lay practitioner is an experiment in Buddhism." What do you think? To me it seems our lay teachers are also an experiment.

Answer: There seems to be some bias there. Certainly, in the West so far, the predominant mode is lay practice and lay teachers. Although there's an increasing amount of interest in people wanting to study with monastic teachers, and there's certainly a strong interest in monastic training, the monastic presence is still pretty tiny, really.

At Abhayagiri, we almost always have a waiting list for people who want to come and train.

The classic model is for the monastic sangha to be laying the foundation for teaching, leadership and being an example. I think oftentimes there is a false dichotomy perceived from the West, because the monastic presence is so strong in Asia. Oftentimes, people overlook the strength of the tradition of lay practice and lay teachers in Asia. Certainly in Thailand, that is very much the case. There are laymen and laywomen who are excellent scholars, teachers. It's not as monochromatic as people perceive.

Look at the model that the Buddha himself gave. There's a very interesting discourse where Māra comes, right after the Buddha is enlightened, and says, "You've done your work; it's time to pack it in. You can die now." And the Buddha says, "It is my function and purpose to teach and I won't pass away until the monks, nuns, laymen, and laywomen are well established in the path and the fruits, able to give leadership and solve problems, able to stand on their own, so this Dhamma and Discipline can last for a long time." That was the Buddha's standard of what was a balanced, strong dispensation: when monks, nuns, laymen, and laywomen were all knowledgeable and well-practiced (D 16).

Q: This is a common scenario: I'm caught in a story of praise and blame. I notice a voice says, "That was very quick. You're getting good at this." I wake up again. "Ah, I know you, Māra." A voice says, "Excellent, what a skillful yogi you're becoming." Māra seems to co-opt every moment of awakening to feed the ego. Do I patiently endure, and this will dissipate with time and practice, or is there something you can suggest?

A: Well, it's both, in the sense that it's really hard to overestimate how important patient endurance is to the practice – the willingness to bear with the pathetic nature of the mind. But then there are also those experiments, those reflections we use in undermining the perceptions of self and ego – the recollection of impermanence, uncertainty, and change. "These are mental states arising and ceasing." That's tuning into it as *dhammas* arising and ceasing, as opposed to me struggling with Māra, me being the champion over Māra, me being defeated by Māra again: that "me and Māra" story.

So, seeing *dhammas* arising and ceasing, that's all that is needed. There isn't a "me" in that. It's a really important aspect of insight to be turning attention towards. Also, we can develop the deconstructing of the process of how thoughts arise and cease: getting to know the sense of feeling, perception, mental formation, consciousness, desire, attachment, and clinging, the process of Dependent

Origination –"It's just these five khandhas that are arising and ceasing"– and being able to rest in the awareness of those five khandhas, as opposed to buying into the story of "me and my khandhas."

Q: The loving-kindness chant includes "May I abide in freedom from affliction." Why is affliction not included in the wish for all beings, while hostility, ill will and anxiety are in both?

A: The reason is because in that chant it's actually just a little bit further down. I can't remember how it's translated, but that particular chant is the chant for all the brahmavihāras: loving-kindness, compassion, sympathetic joy, and equanimity. The wish "May all beings be free from affliction" is an expression of compassion and is actually worded, "May all beings be released from all suffering." That is how it is expressed, because that is the fundamental expression of compassion. The loving-kindness aspiration is the wish for happiness and well-being and the expression of compassion is the wish for freedom from suffering. For some reason, in that chant, it is folded in with loving-kindness. Sometimes it's difficult to find a hard and fast distinction between the two. In order to experience well-being, then of course one needs to be free from suffering.

Q: This morning you spoke about bringing to mind the mettā-nimitta, the mettā-object. I have some understanding of the feeling of mettā, but no understanding of the mettā-nimitta. Could you explain more fully?

A: It's exactly the same. *Nimitta* is more a generic term for the object. We often associate *nimitta* with some type of light or image. With mindfulness of breathing and concentration, there would be encouragement to develop a sign of light or imagery. But the actual word *nimitta* just means sign. So the sign of metta is the feeling, the actual feeling, emotion within the heart, within experience. That is the nimitta.

It is important to attend to that. If one is looking for something else, or just repeating the phrases, thinking, "This is the mettā-nimitta," or trying to conjure up an image of oneself being suffused with loving-kindness somehow, one can get off track. The feeling itself is the sign, the tangible object that is the basis for unification, which one is able to absorb into. As one experiences and nurtures that, one can allow the mind to unify with the feeling, and that's how it expands and stabilizes.

Q: Can you speak about working with fear and loss of ego identity, fear and death?

A: That's one of the places where loving-kindness is a very skillful meditation and exercise, because that sense of fear easily comes up with the loss of the familiar, with the uncertainty of where to place one's attention. What can one trust as one starts to see? Body: can't rely on that. Feelings, perceptions, thoughts: completely untrustworthy. Consciousness: not a good deal. You look at the world around and . . .

So it's easy to be shaken by the instability and uncertainty of everything, and there can be a fear there, uncertainty, a certain confusion and discombobulation. It's good to be able to recognize that, even if our experience is completely uncertain and unstable, "This particular feeling of loving-kindness is trustworthy. I've experienced that. I've seen that. That's a true feeling within the heart."

There is also the confidence that arises just in virtue, all the things that the Buddha encourages. There isn't anything that the Buddha encourages that is something to be looked on askance, as if it were untrustworthy.

On a certain level, when one first approaches the teachings one can think, "Wow, this is a miserable teaching." Like in the morning chanting: Birth is dukkha, ageing is dukkha, sickness is dukkha, death is dukkha, separation is dukkha, association is dukkha: everything's dukkha.

But then when one investigates: "Well, what does the Buddha actually encourage you to do? What does he lay out as a path of practice and training?" The Noble Eightfold Path. Right view, right intention: association with wisdom. Right speech, right action, right livelihood: virtue. Right effort, right mindfulness, right concentration: peaceful, tranquil states of mind. Well, it's all good. The path is completely associated with the wholesome, the skillful, the uplifting.

Then there are other spiritual attributes we can trust, say, the qualities that are conducive to passing over, transcending, crossing over suffering: the *pāramīs*. Generosity, virtue, renunciation, patience, effort, resolution, truthfulness, loving-kindness, equanimity, wisdom: everything that one could conceive of that is really good. That's what the Buddha encourages and that's what forms the basis for the ability to cross over suffering. The heart is replete with well-being and stability. Recollecting and reminding oneself of what the Buddha encourages us to cultivate and develop: those are all exceedingly beneficial, bright states of mind.

When aspects of fear come up, it's helpful to be able to recognize where they come from. Of course, they come from identification with self, identification with ego, identification with body, identification with mind, identification with the world and all the things that we have pretty much no control over. So when one looks at it quite clearly, one realizes, "Well, I really have very little control." It's a very practical teaching to allow us to approach this. It's quite natural in the human condition to be dismayed at the loss of, the threat to, self and ego.

There's a wonderful quote by Ajahn Mahā Boowa, speaking about Ajahn Mun. Ajahn Mun once taught, "Normally, as human beings, we respond to teachings on liberation and nibbāna with a curious sense of fear and trepidation. I don't want to go there. I don't want to do that. There's nothing there. Our parents and grandparents have all taught us quite well to attach to family, attach to possessions, and attach to position." That's our conditioning. As the conditioning changes, inevitably there is a shift that takes place, and I think it is important to recollect what the Buddha actually encourages us to do. This is good stuff.

Q: I'm not sure within the context of this retreat when to be resting simply with the four foundations of mindfulness, and when to be reciting mettā phrases. Can you please advise as to how and when to move skillfully from one practice to the other?

A: Within the context of how I've been presenting what is "billed" as a mettā retreat, there is a recognition of how mettā is a part of a spectrum of practices that are the Buddha's teachings. Certainly the four foundations of mindfulness are an overarching framework to attend to.

There's a discourse where the Buddha talks about establishing mindfulness on particular skillful, wholesome thoughts and being able to hold that exclusively for a day, or a night, or a day and a night: establishing the mind in that, discerning what's skillful and unskillful, and then committing to the wholesome thoughts (M19). But then the mind gets tired, so then it's necessary to return to a place of stillness or stability.

One has to recognize clearly and engage skillfully in the recitation of the mettā phrases. It's using a thought process, and, by its very nature, it's easy for it to become repetitious and feel tiring to the mind. Again, it's important to recognize that the recitation of those phrases is to be used as a recollection and a reminder of the actual feeling. As one establishes that feeling, which is non-discursive, the mind can stay with that. But the recitation is a helpful tool to keep the mind within the bounds of mettā, the loving-kindness perception.

But if one is continuing to do that and the feeling is not strong enough to enable one to rest in it in a non-discursive way, then it's important to rest the mind on an object within the four foundations of mindfulness – body, feeling, mind, and objects of mind – in some way. Of course, the body is an immediate non-discursive object that the mind can rest in, relax in, bringing a settling quality throughout the body and mind. When the mind is refreshed, then it can go back to the recitation to keep developing and stabilizing the perception of the feeling. So, one can work with them back and forth. There's no hard and fast rule. It's more: What is the result? What is the state of the mind? What is going to be useful for settling and stilling?

Q: It seems that mettā would be much easier without a self to protect. How does one realize anattā?

A: That's an excellent question, in the sense that, as an insight, one starts by realizing that the obstruction to mettā is actually not anger and ill will, but the sense of self. That's the big obstruction, and as we reflect, investigate and start having a clear insight into the nature of Dhamma, the nature of the teachings and what the Buddha is giving us as an opportunity for liberation, then loving-kindness is a natural expression of that not-self aspect of the Dhamma. Yes, the cultivation of mettā would be a lot easier without the perception of self.

Q: What is *upekkhā*, equanimity, and how does one practice it?

A: Upekkhā is equanimity and evenness of the mind, the mind being in perfect balance, a sense of recognition of the nature of *kamma*. The practice and basis of equanimity is traditionally described as understanding the nature of *kamma*. The chants we do say: "All beings are the owners of their *kamma*, heir to their *kamma*, born of their *kamma*, related to their *kamma*, abide supported by their *kamma*. Whatever *kamma* they shall do, for good or for ill, of that they will be the heir." The sense of equanimity is being able to recognize that whatever anybody is experiencing is because of causes and conditions that have been laid down.

The stain or "near enemy" of equanimity is indifference. Equanimity is the ability to be very steady and clear, and be in a place of equipoise and balance. One recognizes that the way things work is through causes and conditions, and there's not a "self" involved in it, there's not an individual, it's merely collections of causes and conditions.

Our habit of mind is to go to this person, that individual, that personality, our preferences, our likes and our dislikes. But stepping back to a place of equanimity is being able to see these causes and conditions, so one is not shaken by anything. But it is important to recognize that indifference is not equanimity.

Also, the brahmavihāras are not separate, individual things, like you only have equanimity because you've given up on loving-kindness, compassion, and sympathetic joy. Because loving-kindness and compassion are exceedingly strong and stable, one has increased understanding and insight, so that one is able to rest in a place of complete stability and not be shaken by anything, because one sees that the nature of all things is to arise through causes and conditions.

The reflection on *kamma* is that all beings inherit the results of their *kamma*. There's not a personality, a "me" or "mine." It's not fixed. It isn't as if something happens and then that inevitable, immutable state of being is going to exist forever. Everything is in a state of change. Patterns and circumstances can all change. As one recognizes that and has a much clearer insight into the nature of what causes and conditions are functioning, then one has an opportunity to put attention onto the place where it is going to make the most difference.

Q: What is the most fun part about being a monk?

A: I can assure you it's not fun. It's like eating and sleeping. It's very ordinary. Probably in terms of the most delight or joy that comes is the opportunity to meet really accomplished and pure beings. Fun for a monk is the opportunity to draw close to people and to serve them, or to be in situations where one has contact. You get to meet some exceptional beings.

Q: What does "the four pairs, the eight kinds of noble beings," in the Recollection of the Sangha, mean?

A: It's a way of classification in terms of entry into realization. There are four stages of realization: stream-enterer, once-returner, non-returner, and fully enlightened being, or arahant. *Sotāpanna, sakadāgāmi, anāgāmi,* arahant. So there's four.

Then there's path and fruition. So there are those who are on the path to stream-entry and those who have reached its fruition, those who are on the path to once-returning and those who have reached its fruition, those who are on the path to non-returning and its fruition, and those who are on the path to arahantship and its fruition. Those are the four pairs and eight kinds of noble beings.

In the commentarial tradition, the way they line it up is that the path and fruition are tied to each other. There's a realization of path, and, within mind-moments, there's a realization of fruition. There are a few suttas in the Canon, however, that make it clear that, for someone who is on the path, it could be a long period of time, years even, before there is a fruition. To me, that makes sense.

The sutta tradition has a clear description that there are those who have got an insight into what the path is, what the practice is, what the actual goal is, but who are still yet to have the full realization of that. It could be a very quick insight and realization, or it could take time for that to come to fruition. Those are the four pairs, the eight kinds of noble beings. It *is* a bit mysterious when we chant it.

Q: When doubt is mentioned under the hindrances, is it mainly referring to doubt about the Buddha's teachings? Are there other implications?

A: Oftentimes, when one reads the texts and commentaries, inevitably they talk about doubt about the Buddha's teachings. I and most of the teachers that I know don't narrow it down that much.

In terms of a hindrance, a *nīvaraṇa,* a quality of mind that obstructs the fundamental goodness the mind, then it isn't just doubt about the Buddha's teachings. It's the tendency to doubt, to waver. Of course, when you doubt, waver, or are uncertain, then the focus will be on the teachings, but you'll tend to doubt everything else as well.

So it's good to get a handle on doubt, uncertainty, wavering: how it plays itself out in day-to-day life. It's really interesting to watch on a day-to-day basis. How does it play out? "Should I have two of those fruits or should I just have one? It can turn into a moment where everything stops: should I do this or should I do that; go forward or go back?" We start to doubt everything, doubt can creep into everything and then it manifests in the teachings as well: doubting the teachings, doubting the practice, doubting oneself. "Can I do it? Can I not do it? Is there any point even to doing this? I'm not sure that I can do this." All of it is doubt. So, being able to recognize that it's doubt, and that's all it is, one can then go forward.

This is also a situation where mindfulness of the body is really helpful, in the sense that you're never going to talk yourself into a resolution of doubt through the mind. You'll never get everything figured out enough not to doubt, if doubt is the underlying, fallback position. Recognize how doubt manifests as a feeling of uncertainty, a feeling of hesitation, a feeling of discomfort around a particular decision or action. Then, by employing mindfulness of the body, you can cut through that and move forward. Sometimes it's helpful to make a wrong decision and do something, at least not get caught in wavering and uncertainty, just as a part of training. That sense of wanting to be absolutely sure that one is doing something right before doing it paralyzes you and ties you up in knots. So, be willing to cut through that and move forward. One can feel in the body that it is helpful just to move forward, to take action, and not get caught in doubt.

Mettā and Relinquishment

For loving-kindness to manifest fully and come to
fruition, we need to undermine the fundamental
roots of attachment, defilement, and clinging.

A couple of people astutely noticed that I had skipped a few lines of the *Mettā Sutta*. I consciously did that because I wanted to take the time to address them. I had spent pretty much the full hour talking about the *Mettā Sutta* up to that point, and I thought, "I don't want to open up this can of worms and go on longer."

The *Mettā Sutta* lays the basis and foundation of the cultivation of mettā in terms of conduct, speech, and how we live in the world. It then goes into the actual cultivation of loving-kindness, giving different parameters, guidelines, and encouragement, saying we should sustain the recollection of mettā, which "is said to be the sublime abiding."

The sutta ends with, "By not holding to fixed views, the pure-hearted one, having clarity of vision, being freed from all sense desires, is not born again into this world." With just a cursory glance, we might think, "How did that get tacked on? That doesn't have anything to do with mettā." But I think that we actually bring mettā to complete fruition by having the insight and understanding not to be caught in views, opinions, and attachment to our perspectives.

"Being freed from all sense desires" is a radical relinquishing of attachment. For loving-kindness to manifest fully and come to fruition, we need to undermine the fundamental roots of attachment, defilement, and clinging.

So this takes mettā practice and ramps it up to another level, bringing it to a liberating insight practice. As we cultivate loving-kindness, the heart becomes more attuned to its own movement. We start to feel the movement within the heart more clearly.

Wanting to take a fixed view or have a position involves a feeling of contention and conflict, a feeling of butting up against something or somebody. How do we deal with that? Do we just swamp it with loving-kindness and make it go away? That is one way.

Or, do we say, "Well, what's the root of that? What's the root of that feeling, of having to hold a view of right or wrong . . . good or bad . . . this is correct . . . this is incorrect . . . it's got to be this way?" What is the root of that? The root is the sense of self, of "I am." The mettā practice is a very skillful means of softening and opening the heart, so that it's able to tune in and say, "Well, that's suffering." Even if your view is correct, holding it with a sense of self is still suffering!

We prop up views and positions and then land in places of suffering. "I had such loving-kindness going. How did I get back to this point of suffering again?" That is the way it works when there is still greed, hatred, and delusion, when there are still the underlying roots of the āsavas, the outflows. In order for mettā to come to fruition, we need to shine a light on the deeper-rooted tendencies.

How do we work with them? Of course, one of the ways of working with them is with loving-kindness, in the sense that if we set ourselves up in opposition with our minds, then we are in a constant state of conflict. So, the kindest act that we can do is to let go of defilement and attachment. That is the kindest thing we can do for ourselves and others. We use the cultivation of loving-kindness as a means of highlighting where we create opposition and conflict, where we hold to a particular view, and how significant views are in supporting negative underlying tendencies within the mind.

The Buddha outlined the three outflows (āsavas), as sensual desire (kāmāsava), becoming (bhavāsava), and ignorance (avijjāsava—not knowing, not having true knowledge). Very soon after the Buddha's passing, commentators added the outflow of views (diṭṭhāsava) because it seemed fundamental as well. These are a source of suffering and also perpetuate the round of rebirth.

Views are deeply rooted in the mind. Even if they are not argumentative views, they still involve having to take a position, having to be right or wrong. In the Buddha's time, there was a whole list of standard views that are probably not so meaningful to us. But at the Buddha's time, they were the philosophical positions of the day. There were schools of religious seekers and philosophers who took various positions. Is the cosmos eternal or not eternal? What is the nature of the self? What is the nature of the body and the mind? Do enlightened beings exist after death? Do they not exist after death? Do they both exist and not exist after death? Or, do they neither exist nor not exist after death?

There were great philosophical debates and conflicts about this. In a more modern setting, well, pick your view of choice.

There is a discourse (A 10:96) in which Ānanda goes into a wanderer's park around Rājagaha and goes to a hot springs. He meets a wanderer, who immediately starts questioning him:

"What teacher do you follow?"
   "I follow the son of the Sakyans, Gotama."
   "What view do you hold? That the world is eternal, this alone is true, anything else is wrong?"
   "I don't hold to such a view, friend."
   "The world is not eternal; this alone is true, anything else is wrong?"
   "I don't hold to such a view, friend."

The wanderer runs through the entire litany of positions and Ānanda responds with each one, "I don't hold such a view, friend."

The wanderer is perplexed with this and asks, "Could it be that you don't know or see?" Ānanda assures him that he does know and see (an idiom for insight). What he knows and sees is that all these different views are just speculative views. By understanding the foundation of views, the obsession with views, the origination of views, and the uprooting of views, there is a true knowing and seeing.

It's a wonderful perspective on views, opinions, and attachments. To be accomplished in not having views, one doesn't have to become a kind of space cadet, completely out there, incapable of answering a question. But by recognizing how one starts to fix oneself into a position, and seeing, "Oh, I'm putting myself in opposition to that person or to that situation by holding to that view and that's going to lead to suffering," then one is able to step back from that position of holding to views. That allows one to return to a place of mindfulness and clear comprehension or discernment. That is what one takes as one's abiding place.

We recognize that whatever comes up is just a mental formation within the mind, just a thought or just a perception. We can have a perception about something and realize that it's impermanent, unsatisfactory, and not-self. Sometimes we can act on views or perceptions if they have a usefulness at that particular time, but we are not building our home or sense of self within that.

To tie that in again with loving-kindness: it's being very kind to yourself and others because it doesn't take very long to recollect the last time you were at loggerheads with somebody because of a particular view. You think about it afterwards and wonder, "Why did I even go there? What was the point of that anyway?"

If we are not trapped by views, usually we can respond quite skillfully, and that is exceedingly useful. Reflect on the sense of non-contention as a basis for loving-kindness. There is an idiom in the scriptural language that describes this mental state of attaching to views: "This alone is true, anything else is wrong." It isn't as if we have consciously thought this out or even articulated it within the mind, but it is there. We can change our views, but at that particular moment it feels like, "This is right and everything else is wrong."

As soon as we are in that kind of position, it's the basis for contention and conflict. It's the basis for feeling irritation and aversion, whether short or protracted. Ill will is going to be attendant on holding that particular view.

Try to make this very conscious through the cultivation of loving-kindness so as not to allow the formation of views to be so strong. Have a sense of loving-kindness and well-wishing towards yourself because you are usually the first person to suffer when you are tightly locked into a particular view. Then, of course, others suffer as well.

The active application of loving-kindness is not just a nice emotion that we are able to generate sometimes while we are sitting on our cushions. It's a very practical application of how we can interface with the world around us and not be trapped by fixed views. It lays the basis for peace and clarity.

One of the underlying principles of the Dhamma that the Buddha pointed to is this aspect of letting go, relinquishing, and putting down. We can let go: we can let go of a mood, irritation, or aversion; we can let go of a view that's starting to arise; we can let go of a particular perspective of how I think it has to be; we can let go of sense desires; and we can let go of the whole construct of "I am." It's that letting go that allows us to access and experience a real peace.

There are a few places in the discourses in which the Buddha is asked for a way to formulate these teachings in a very succinct way. In the scriptures the Buddha says that all *dhammas—sabbe dhammā*—are not to be clung to, all *dhammas* are not worthy of holding on to, all *dhammas* are not to be attached to. All things, all *dhammas* with a small "d," are not worthy of clinging. That's a very simple phrase that's helpful for practice, especially in terms of mettā-bhāvanā. If we get entangled in the obstructions that come up in the mind or try to analyze and figure them out too much, they hook us in.

The answer is to be able to come from that place of "all things are not to be clung to." Maybe there is a mood of distraction, irritation, or confusion, but all *dhammas* are not to be clung to. Then we need to bring into being the cultivation of loving-kindness, which is an expansive, wholesome quality that we ultimately have to let go of. But again, it's a useful bridge to putting our effort and attention into things that help establish and sustain a sense of peace and clarity. So, the act of letting go is a very useful tool.

One of the places that this teaching comes up is in a very interesting discourse, a well-known teaching that most people who have been on a meditation retreat have probably heard referred to in one way or another. It's the discourse given to Moggallāna when he was meditating and experiencing drowsiness (A 7:61). It was shortly after Moggallāna was ordained. He is practicing diligently but is being overcome by drowsiness, sloth, and torpor. The Buddha comes and gives him instruction.

That set of instructions is, first, to make your object of meditation clear. If that doesn't work, then use an image of light to bring brightness to the mind. Use a recitation if that image of brightness doesn't work. If that doesn't work, pull your ears, rub your skin, and get some energy going somehow. If that doesn't work, go out and look at the sky, look at the stars. If that doesn't work, do some walking meditation. In the end, if none of this works, then lie down and have a rest, mindfully establishing a time for getting up and continuing your practice.

The Buddha continues on and gives Moggallāna instruction in being careful not to get too involved with or to draw too close to laypeople, because laypeople have busy lives, and if you're trying to be a part of their lives and they ignore you, then you wonder, "Oh, what did I do wrong?" There are endless complications. You're a monk, do what monks do. Let laypeople do what laypeople do. Don't get too entangled in other people's lives.

Then the Buddha gives Moggallāna instruction in maintaining a sense of circumspection in speech because inevitably, a lot of conversation and talking ends up in a lot of conflict. There are always misunderstandings. Restrain yourself in speech, paying attention to maintaining humility and not being proud wherever you go or whatever you do: good instructions for a new monk.

Then Moggallāna asks the Buddha, "What is the core of the teachings? What is their basis?" That's when the Buddha says that the fundamental teaching is that all *dhammas* are not to be clung to. When you don't cling to things, you are not building the momentum of habits and attachments. When you are not building that momentum of habits and attachments, you are not creating a sense of being sustained by them. When you are not being sustained by all those habit patterns, then you can dwell free and unsustained within the world and the body-mind complex. It's a wonderful teaching. It's very, very direct.

As we reflect and investigate, we see how views—attachments to a sense of self, our sense of what we think is right and wrong, how things should and shouldn't be—are endlessly frustrating, agitating, and a source of dukkha. The Buddha's perspective is not that we are trying to wipe it all out and annihilate it, but rather that we are trying to understand the reason why we take a position or view. We are seeing the dynamic of that movement of mind that has to have a position of: "I am . . . I am right . . . I am wrong . . . I am good . . . I am not good . . . I'm correct . . . I'm wrong again"—all the positions that we take.

The word "conceit" in Buddhism has a whole level of meaning different from the way we normally use it in the English language. According to the teachings, there are nine different bases of conceit:

1. being inferior and assuming oneself to be inferior

2. being inferior and assuming oneself to be equal

3. being inferior and assuming oneself to be superior

4. being equal and assuming oneself to be inferior

5. being equal and assuming oneself to be equal

6. being equal and assuming oneself to be superior

7. being superior and assuming oneself to be inferior

8. being superior and assuming oneself to be equal

9. being superior and assuming oneself to be superior.

All of that is the basis of conceit. This is the act of trying to take a position all the time.

You realize all of that is suffering: trying to figure out "Who am I? Where am I?" in this realm of relating to myself in the world around me and in comparison to others. As soon as you go there, you're trapped.

So again, bring it back to kindness, mettā: "May I abide in well-being; may all beings abide in well-being." That is a much safer position, being able to drop and set aside all the "I"-making and "my"-making. This "I"-making and "my"-making is constantly being constructed; it isn't as if the "I, me, and mine" is related to an actual fixed entity.

This is something we are doing all of the time. That is made really clear in the Pali words ahaṅkāra and mamaṅkāra. Kāra is the verb "to do": the "I-doing" and "mine-doing." We are doing it and creating it, although it's like the sorcerer's apprentice in Walt Disney's Fantasia. The apprentice ends up with a lot of complications and far more than he bargained for.

The teachings of the Buddha give us the tools to be able to allow that to be let go of, to be put down, to be dropped. Of course that is a "doing" as well, but part of the practice is the craft of placing attention. We need to be doing something. On a certain level, we are doing something all the time. It's just the nature of the body and mind. But we can put attention on the act of relinquishment, the act of kindness. Those are very conscious acts that reap the fruits of well-being and peace.

We need to remind ourselves to do this: "One should sustain this recollection." It's reminding ourselves and recollecting mindful application. As we relinquish, "not holding to fixed views, the pure hearted one, having clarity of vision, being freed from all sense desire, is not born again into this world." Somebody who is freed from all sense desires and is not born again into this world is an *anāgāmi* or arahant, a non-returner or somebody who is a fully enlightened being. That's a real act of kindness, to be somebody who is fully able to penetrate the teachings and to be completely free of the entanglements of samsara.

Of course, the example closest to me, a contemporary example, is Ajahn Chah. The Buddha's example is still resonating after 2,500 years. The act of relinquishment, being able to be freed from all sense desires, turning away from the cycle of samsara, has had an extraordinarily powerful effect on the world.

Ajahn Chah set an example of loving-kindness and had the ability to inspire people to practice. I don't know exactly how many monasteries in Thailand are affiliated with Ajahn Chah—several hundred. And, of course, there is the Western Sangha: America, Canada, England, France, Switzerland, Germany, Italy, New Zealand, Australia, and Malaysia. Monasteries and so many other places have grown up just from this small bullfrog of a man. It's like he sat on his lily pad in the middle of this monastery, and everybody came to him.

Ajahn Chah's loving-kindness was one that came to fruition through commitment to relinquishment. When he was asked, "What seems to have made the difference to you?" he said, "Well, I always wanted to find an end to things." He wasn't satisfied until he really found an end.

Ajahn Chah had a lot of difficulty in practice. It wasn't easy for him. On a certain level, that probably made him a lot more kind and compassionate, since he could definitely take in the foibles of the rest of us. He had the ability to see through. He cultivated loving-kindness, but it isn't as if he didn't have to deal with his own anger, aversion, or ill will.

There is a nice story about Ajahn Chah. He was sitting and teaching, as often happened, underneath his dwelling place. A palm reader (an astrologer) was visiting and was captivated by his humor and warmth. He finally screwed up the courage to ask Ajahn Chah if he could look at the lines on his hands. Of course, Ajahn Chah teased him and said, "Well, am I going to win the lottery?" The palm reader looked at his hands and said, "Luang Por, the lines in your hands—you've got a lot of anger!" Ajahn Chah smiled and said, "Yes, but I don't use it." It's those simple words: you don't negate personality or temperament, but you have the wisdom and the clarity to say: "I really don't want to repeat that. Been there, done that. Time to let it go."

Another story about Ajahn Chah took place when he had already been abbot of the monastery for some years. He was a real taskmaster. If you talk to the really senior monks, you would find out it was not much fun; he was very strict. One day, after the meal, everyone else had finished and left. As Ajahn Chah was walking past a novice, he saw the novice standing, picking up a kettle, and, rather than going to find a cup, drinking directly from it. Ajahn Chah lost it. In the first place, it is impolite for a monk or novice to stand and drink. And then to do it by drinking straight from the kettle was too much.

Ajahn Chah took one look and just bolted after the lad. He was going to beat this little novice. The novice saw him and was out of there. Ajahn Chah chased after him, trying to catch the novice to thrash him. The novice was quicker and got away. Then it hit Ajahn Chah: what was he doing? He went back to his dwelling place and didn't come out for three days. He sat and worked with that anger. He didn't come out, go on almsround, or eat. The monks said that after that occasion, nobody ever saw him display anger again. It was very, very interesting. He just realized, "This is painful, this is suffering, and I've really got to deal with it."

Teachers who are wise or compassionate aren't born like that—that's not how it works. You have to work at it; you have to deal with it. There needs to be the realization: this is suffering and there is a way out of this. It's seeing that taking rebirth again and again, even if it's pleasant, is not worth it. This is a tremendous gift of kindness to the world. That's something that we can be doing, each in our own way. We can set that intention, that resolution. Mettā-bhāvanā is not an indulgent way of making yourself feel good for a little bit. It's cultivating the roots of your liberation and recognizing what is of benefit to you and all beings. So I offer that for reflection this morning.

Spreading Mettā to the Four Quarters

*Draw attention to loving-kindness and slowly build
momentum, allowing it to take hold within the heart.*

As we work with the cultivation of mettā, loving-kindness, one
cause for the arising of loving-kindness is not attending to things
that are irritating or conducive to aversion. As a conscious cultivation, we pay attention to things we perceive as good or as conducive
to happiness and well-being.

We are making a conscious choice. This doesn't mean that everything is wonderful and beautiful. But: "Do I really want to attend
to things that stir up the quality of aversion and ill will?" By consciously attending to those things that we perceive as conducive
to well-being and supporting the wish of well-being, there is a
strength of intention that forms in the mind, and we are able to
sustain that flow of well-wishing.

In this light, I think it is important to recognize that we don't
need to override or dismiss our faculty of discernment, for this is
what enables us to recognize that there are things conducive to
aversion and ill will. It enables us to not give that aversion so much
playing time in the mind.

In reality, if we wanted to catalog all the things that we are of-
fended and feel disgruntled by, the list could start growing. But
there is a conscious choice not to give it that attention. In recognizing the benefits of mettā, the physical and mental sense of ease
that we experience, we encourage ourselves to direct our attention

to that which is conducive to the welling up within consciousness of thoughts and feelings of loving-kindness.

Likening this to food, there are lots of foods that draw our attention, but if we make our diet cheesecake and junk food, we end up not very healthy. I have a friend in Australia who sent me a picture captioned, "Michelangelo's David returns after two years in America." It's a very funny picture of an obese David. In the same way, the heart needs to be nourished by positive things that brighten the mind and the heart and bring a sense of well-being.

The conscious cultivation of loving-kindness is a skillful way of directing attention. As we do that, it acts almost as a solvent to dissolve and wash away niggling thoughts and moods of aversion and ill will. That has a certain power within consciousness because when we see things in the light of aversion, ill will, and irritation, then everything is an intrusion and source of irritation. Things get read through the lens of irritation.

One of the images that the Buddha uses describing the hindrances is water (A 5.163). When water is left to its own devices, it is clean, pure, cool, satisfying, and refreshing. We can see through it clearly. But the image he gives when he compares it to the hindrance of ill will and aversion is boiling water. It's boiling and bubbling, and we can't see our reflection in it, or see through it clearly. If it bubbles out of the pan and splashes on us, it burns us. Aversion and ill will have that same quality.

As we settle the mind down, bring the mind back to its natural state without adding aversion and ill will, and cool it with the development of mettā, then it returns to a clear, limpid state. It is refreshing to look at, to wash with, and to drink. You can do anything you want with it when the mind is brought to that state.

Recollecting the life of the Buddha as an example of loving-kindness, there are incidents in which he relied on its application and it had a powerful effect. One is the story, toward the end of his life, of his cousin Devadatta, who was also a monk but was very covetous of the Buddha's position and wanted to take over. The Buddha didn't give him much encouragement, and Devadatta developed a grudge against the Buddha and plotted to kill him.

One way he did that was to bribe the king's men who were the keepers of Nālāgiri, the state elephant but also a rogue elephant, whose job description was that of executioner. They plied him with alcohol and let him loose as the Buddha was approaching, so that this enraged elephant would trample the Buddha. Ānanda, the Buddha's trustworthy attendant, saw the elephant coming and jumped in front of the Buddha, wanting to protect him. The Buddha asked him to step aside and then radiated loving-kindness. As the story goes, the elephant came barreling up to the Buddha but then stopped in his tracks, quite close to the Buddha, affected with that power of loving-kindness. It then bowed and used his trunk to gather some dust from the Buddha's feet and put it on his own head (Cv 7.10–12). It's a lovely story and could very well have happened. Even if it didn't, it's still a meaningful story.

Rarely are we faced with raging elephants coming towards us, but the Buddha chose to exercise his trust in the power of loving-kindness. I think, in having contact with day-to-day circumstances, it is very helpful to bring up such images: "If the Buddha can rely in such extreme circumstances on loving-kindness, why don't I give it a try in this circumstance and see what happens?" Generally, you will find that it works. Something changes. It is part of the natural order: all beings respond to loving-kindness.

I remember one instance when I was still living in Thailand. I was fairly young in my role as an abbot and was having a conflict with a few of the monks. There was a constant feeling of agitation and wondering why these "idiots" didn't comply with my "rightness," which was obvious to me. After some time using that method and not being very successful, I thought I'd give loving-kindness a try.

A small group of monks had banded together and were creating a lot of division throughout the community. I decided to start going on a longer alms round, close to an hour and a half, which was the route that they had been going on. The whole period is in silence. Every morning, just before dawn, you walk through the countryside and villages and return to the monastery.

So, I would begin the day going on alms round with them, taking the whole time to visualize, generate, and spread loving-kindness to them. I tried to hold it as clearly as I could throughout the day, but I would make it a particularly strong focus during alms round. It was really interesting. About the third day, those monks started coming to me. Whereas before, communication had completely shut down, they came, we communicated, and it all opened up from there. We were able to discuss and figure out where we had gone off track. It was resolved within just a few days. I found it quite astounding and inspiring.

If you really set your mind to loving-kindness, it has a transformative effect. Of course, the major effect was on myself, not holding to fixed views. That helps a lot. It seems pretty mundane, not as spectacular as stories of the Buddha. If you have experimented with loving-kindness, you will find that you have a story or know somebody who has a story about how it has really worked. If we take the time to cultivate and use it, there will be some kind of effect. This is quite natural. The sense of loving-kindness is a universal quality that we as human beings all respond to.

Today I'd like to introduce another formulation of loving-kindness meditation, based on the one we chanted this morning: "I will abide pervading one quarter with a mind . . ." The chanting book says "heart," but it is usually translated as "mind." For me, it seems to chant a bit more nicely with "mind."

This is the most common formulation of loving-kindness and the brahmavihāras in the discourses. It comes up in many places: "I will abide pervading one quarter . . ."—this is directional in the sense that it is conceived of in terms of the directions, the four quarters—"with a mind imbued with loving-kindness; likewise the second, likewise the third, likewise the fourth; so above and below and around and everywhere; and to all as to myself." The sense is of spreading loving-kindness in the different directions—north, south, east, west, above and below, all around—so that we are allowing the feeling of loving-kindness to expand.

"To all as to myself" establishes that feeling of loving-kindness within the heart, then allows it to pervade and extend. That's the next part of the chant, "I will abide pervading the all-encompassing world with a mind imbued with loving-kindness"—throughout the extension of the world and ultimately all worlds, not just how we conceive of our little planet, floating in space. Allow that sense of extension, that abundant, exalted, and immeasurable quality.

"Without hostility and without ill will": this is the encouragement. Without any hostility, without allowing ill will, is the key to sending or shining forth loving-kindness, as in the introduction to the chant, "Now let us make the four boundless qualities shine forth." We allow the heart and mind to be established in those sublime qualities. Allow it to shine forth, not obstructing it with aversion, ill will, worry, or fear, all the tendencies that we can add to it.

As we do this, we allow the heart to feel abundant, exalted, and immeasurable. We see that these qualities are truly beautiful. When we think of physical beauty in the world, it doesn't compare to the beauty of a sublime quality like loving-kindness. It's an image the Buddha uses. In comparison with the stars, there isn't anything that shines as brightly as the sun. In the same way, there isn't any quality that shines as brightly as loving-kindness. Or at night, there isn't anything that shines as brightly as the full moon. In the same way, there isn't any quality that shines as brightly as loving-kindness.

The Buddha gives various, apt images: nourishing ourselves with those qualities of loving-kindness, pervading above, below, around, and everywhere, to all as to myself. There is the sense of establishing within ourselves this abundant, exalted, and immeasurable feeling.

It wasn't very long after we did the translation of these chants and started chanting them that someone said, "When we do these chants, we are supposed to feel abundant, exalted, and immeasurable, and all I feel is abandoned, exhausted, and miserable." But what is needed is to draw attention to this quality and to slowly build momentum, allowing it to take hold within the heart.

I think we also need to have a tremendous amount of kindness and well-wishing for the habits of our minds. They are so deeply ingrained. Do not be daunted by that. It's all doable; it's all workable. It's drop by drop and little by little. We can establish these qualities and bring them to mind, sowing the seeds. Over time, it definitely grows.

The image that the Thai monks use is that when we are cultivating good qualities and that which is skillful, we have to be willing to be like a farmer sowing rice. He is just throwing seeds away, out into the fields. We are not quite sure whether it is going to grow. What's going to happen? But it's the nature of things that when conditions are ripe and the sun, water, and soil are good, the seeds we "threw away" grow up into plants. They go through that cycle.

Similarly, with our practice of sowing the seeds of loving-kindness in the heart, plugging them into consciousness, we find they come back again. What arises is the sense of spaciousness, warmth, and kindness.

We can use this particular chant as a theme as we sit and bring those thoughts of loving-kindness into being. "To all as to myself": bring one's attention to oneself. Visualize oneself sitting here. Visualize oneself as happy, as if one were looking into a mirror at a time when one was very happy, feeling well, comfortable, and at ease. Bring that into mind, into consciousness. "Here I am sitting here, happy, at ease, free from fear, ill will, and anxiety." Just allow that to establish itself.

Then use the phrases: "May I be well and happy; may I retain this feeling of happiness and well-being." Allow it to settle and pervade the body. Breathe it in so it pervades from the top of the head down. In just the same sense that the breath energizes the body, the feeling of loving-kindness energizes, brightens, relaxes, and softens the head, the top of the head, the neck, and shoulders.

Breathe out, relaxing any tension, any feeling of conflict or difficulty. Allow it to release. Breathe in, allowing the warmth of loving-kindness to pervade the shoulders, the arms, relaxing and softening the whole chest, back, and abdomen. Softening but energizing and brightening: that is the nature of loving-kindness energy. The lower back, the legs, the knees, and down to the soles of the feet: use the energy of loving-kindness to establish it in oneself.

Again, we use those thoughts or reminders, whether it is planting the seed with just one word of mettā or some other formulation that may strike a chord, "Wishing gladness and safety: May all beings be at ease. May I be well and happy." Whatever works. We are not trying to be technically correct. Rather, what is actually going to work and be helpful?

Feel your way through it. Allow your sense of loving-kindness to establish itself within the heart and within this being. Then allow that feeling to expand, pervade, and suffuse. It's helpful not to be too ambitious in the beginning. If you are using the different quarters, pervade one quarter with the mind imbued with loving-kindness. You can just take it to five, ten, or twenty feet around you.

Pervade one quarter: the north. What's in front of you? What's on the eastern side, the right-hand side? What's in the south, behind you? On the western, left-hand side? "Above, below, around, and everywhere, and to all as to myself." Allow that to stabilize and feel comfortable. Breathe into that space. Allow the breath energy and the energy of loving-kindness to pervade that space, however you conceive of it in your mind—starting small, near and around you.

Allow that feeling not to be obstructed by discursive thought or the sense of "Am I doing this wrong? Am I doing it right?" Don't analyze or think about it. This is a feeling exercise. Allow that sense of pervading space with a mind imbued with loving-kindness, what-ever it is and however you have conceived of it, five or ten feet around you.

"Abundant, exalted, immeasurable, and to all as to myself, with-out hostility and without ill will." These are reminders to keep it bright and clear. Allow it to stabilize. Then use the phrase again: "I will abide pervading one quarter with a mind imbued with loving-kindness."

Extend the feeling to whatever feels comfortable. We are in a valley, so pervade the valley with loving-kindness, sitting here. What's in front? All the people, all the beings, whether they are hu-man beings, people in our group, people that are residents here; the animals that are here; the beings that are non-material, any earth devas, any other beings that are here. Extend loving-kindness, in-cluding all beings.

The second quarter to the east or off to one's right: all those beings in that quarter; those who are in the south, who are behind one; those who are on one's left-hand side. Allow that to extend, becoming more expansive and brightening.

There is the sense that all beings are worthy of our loving-kindness. All beings appreciate it. When we meet somebody who gives us a gesture of kindness, it's always appreciated. It's natu-ral. So we sit and generate, spread, suffuse, and pervade the space around the four quarters, above and below, around and every-where. Allow that to become brighter and brighter.

Do not allow yourself to be held back by feelings of limitation. We limit ourselves with our perception of being unable, unworthy, or not good enough. We realize that is not necessary. With loving-kindness, it really doesn't apply. It's such a universal quality; allow that to pervade. "I will abide pervading the all-encompassing world with a mind imbued with loving kindness; abundant, exalted, im-measurable, without hostility, and without ill will."

Recognize that even if it is just a niggling bit of ill will, a flash of negativity, it's a limitation of the heart that can be set aside and dropped. We can allow that feeling of loving-kindness to expand. We can continue working with it; we can experiment. Allow the feeling of loving-kindness to extend further out, to more and more beings, not making any distinction, not dividing the world up into us and them or me and others. Recognize that the heart of loving-kindness doesn't make those distinctions. That is its fundamental quality. That is what gives it its strength, when we're able not to get bogged down in those distinctions. As we make those distinctions—me and others, us and them—that limitation and feeling of constriction is immediately felt.

If you feel the suffusion of loving-kindness collapsing, just start back again. Direct loving-kindness to yourself: "And to all as to myself." Attend to those thoughts of loving-kindness directed to yourself. That is the seed, the core, the base that we work from.

There is a teacher in Thailand whose primary teaching tool and methodology is the cultivation of loving-kindness. Sometimes he will have people work towards the establishing of loving-kindness to themselves and won't encourage them to go beyond that, for a year, two years, three years. Just keep working on that. That's the core. Don't get ambitious until you can lay that base and establish it solidly within yourself.

As an exercise, it is interesting to see what happens to the mind as we allow loving-kindness to expand and pervade. Again, if you feel there is some obstruction coming up, reestablish that there is no rush to go anywhere. The main object of the contemplation or meditation is to establish mettā, the object of loving-kindness within the heart. And that's what we allow to grow, nourishing and supporting that.

If we are able to extend that feeling outward and find that it is useful for our cultivation, all well and good. But again, pay attention to the experience, investigating, "Is it useful? Is it working? Is it helpful?" "I will abide, pervading the all-encompassing world with a mind imbued with loving-kindness; abundant, exalted, immeasurable, without hostility and without ill will."

Questions and Answers

Question: Realized beings abound these days. Care to comment? When the conditions are conducive and the inquiry is in earnest, is it possible to "wake up" quickly?

Answer: I remember when Ajahn Chah came to America to teach. Because he had done some traveling and had taught in a few different places, he was asked, "Now that you have been in America for a while, how do you feel about Buddhism coming to America?" Ajahn Chah had this blank look on his face and said that Buddhism hadn't come to America yet: "I haven't seen any Buddhism yet." Ajahn Chah could be naughty sometimes.

Certainly, when the conditions are conducive and the inquiry is in earnest, it is possible to wake up quickly, but finding conducive conditions and having that earnest inquiry is not that easy. You really have to sustain inquiry and be focused, which is not that easy.

Much of Ajahn Chah's teaching is around endurance because that is what is required. We all tend to set the intention to wake up quickly when we first start practicing. I ordained with the idea that I would take a temporary ordination, learn about meditation (I had three or four spare months) and achieve stream-entry at least. Then I could go do what I wanted. I wouldn't have to be reborn in the lower realms again. It's not quite that easy, but certainly, attention to conducive conditions and the earnestness of inquiry are really important.

Q: Which suttas describe path and fruit?

A: There are two different modalities. One is the path as I described it the other night. There is also another kind of modality, a seven-factor description of path and realization. That is in *Majjhima Nikāya* 70, the *Kīṭāgiri Sutta*. Path and fruit are fairly ubiquitous, but I don't have a good reference off the top of my head.

Q: Would you say a bit about the benefits of dwelling in loving-kindness during the dying process? Both for the caregiver and the person dying.

A: The immediate benefit for the person dying is that the mind is not drawn to negative mental states. That eases the whole process of dying. There is physical ease and the diminution of fear. One is able to pass away and let the body go with clarity because it is held within the sphere of loving-kindness. That's a tremendous benefit.

For the caregiver, there is the ability to retain and dwell in the perspectives of loving-kindness. It is very tiring looking after a dying body, so there are endless amounts of frustration and uncertainty. Dwelling in loving-kindness is a way to ameliorate some of the frustrations, worries, fears, and projections that come. Sometimes we overextend ourselves, trying to be the ideal caregiver. To be able to say with loving-kindness, "I'm really fried. You need to ask somebody else to help out," is itself an act of loving-kindness.

These bodies are high maintenance when they don't work. In the last nine years of Ajahn Chah's life, he was unable to look after himself. He was bedridden and unable to speak or use his limbs. It was a wonderful opportunity for the monks to be able to look after him. They set things up extraordinarily well. There would be four monks and a novice in the daytime and four monks and a novice at night, fully looking after all of his needs. There would be a very experienced monk as a head caregiver overseeing everything.

Every two weeks there would be a change. People would come to Ajahn Chah's monastery and wait in line to care for him. They wouldn't do anything for Ajahn Chah that they hadn't become proficient at. As it got to the later stages, with nasal feeding tubes, monks had to train and practice on themselves before they were allowed to get close to Ajahn Chah. He was bedridden for nine years and never had a bedsore, which is quite extraordinary. That level of care was done out of gratitude and loving-kindness. It was a real honor to be able to look after him.

But most people do not have a huge sangha of monks. It's hard work to look after bodies that are breaking down. One of the uses of loving-kindness is being realistic as to how we need to be kind to ourselves and draw other people in as well. Often we feel that we should be doing everything. It's like the horse in George Orwell's *Animal Farm*, "I will work harder. I will work harder." And of course the pigs keep piling on the work. The horse collapses, dies, and is shipped off to the glue factory. It is really important to have loving-kindness about our limits and to find other resources.

Q: If everything about me, my body, thoughts, feelings, and consciousness is impermanent, and even if my "self" is illusionary, whom or what am I addressing when I wish myself well-being?

A: It isn't as if there is no one home. This conventional self is a focal point, has taken rebirth, has a mind, and has results ripening from the past. These aren't illusory in the sense that they have no meaning or effect. We experience and feel those results. Part of the means of disentangling ourselves and ceasing to suffer from the complications that we make of that self is loving-kindness. It is one of the skillful means for amelioration.

The negation of self is just as much a wrong view as the full-blown belief in self. There is a narrow balance that we need to make in order to understand the teachings. This is not a nihilistic teaching. That is one of the fundamental wrong views that the Buddha points to as a source of suffering: being caught up in the self and what we perceive as self, but also the negation and the tendency to annihilation of self. That is also a wrong view that leads to suffering.

There is a very real cause-and-effect process going on. We feel and experience the results of actions and the skillful application of that which is positive, wholesome, and leads to peace, clarity, and well-being. These are exceedingly useful.

Q: For most of the time on this retreat I have had a lot of thoughts and worries about a problem that I have been dealing with in daily life and which I will have to continue to deal with after the retreat. I've tried to work skillfully with it, extending mettā to myself and the others involved and doing mindfulness practice, working with anxiety, anger, aversion, playing out all the possible scenarios, and returning to the body. This only seems to intensify things and feels obsessional. I recognize this pattern from numerous prior retreats, although the thematic content changes. I'm feeling discouraged. Any suggestions?

A: I think one of the things is recognizing that this is the way the mind tends to go. It grabs a particular scenario or difficulty and then obsesses on it. There is anxiety and fear around it. It's good to be able to say, "Okay, that's a reasonably well-established pattern," and be able to recognize that. It's better to approach it by asking, "Can I have loving-kindness for that tendency to follow and be in that pattern?" rather than trying to think, "I need loving-kindness for myself; I need loving-kindness for that person," and parcel it all out.

The ideal is to bring a sense of kindness and well-wishing to that pattern and see how the mind loops into those reactions. It helps to give it some space, seeing the particular habit or pattern, and then stepping back from the identification with it and recognizing it is an object worthy of well-wishing.

When we relate to ourselves, our habit patterns, our temperament and personality, we're often not extraordinarily kind. We tend to have higher expectations and a lower level of patience. If you were your close friend, would you respond in the same way? Take the same scenario, but place a good friend in the spot where you perceive yourself. With that same scenario and circumstances, what would be your response?

You would find that the response would be almost invariably much kinder and more patient, spacious, forgiving, and generous. That's a very helpful exercise in imagination or visualization: just to replace yourself with somebody else. Recognize that you would probably respond in a completely different way.

Q: Was Ajahn Chah an *anāgāmi* (non-returner) when he became angry with the young monk? I thought the root of anger is uprooted at that stage. Please explain.

A: Absolutely not, with that kind of anger. An anāgāmi has absolutely eradicated anger and sensual desire. That was the sign that he really missed his shot and still had some major defilements to work with, and that's what he put his energy into working with.

Q: Would you explain the meaning of the Pali blessings you chant after the meal offering? I can't remember the whole translation but remember that it is very beautiful and complements the concept of mettā.

A: I can't remember it either, truth be told. One of the reasons that we don't do it in English is that we haven't got a really good translation of it. We have tried on various occasions. It is either hokey or clunky, so we haven't been able to get it into English. But essentially, the chant is a recognition of the goodness that has been done. One of the images is that as water wells up and overflows, goodness spreads forth. Recognize the goodness that is done, and, by the power of that goodness, may you be free from difficulty and illness. May you receive the blessings of goodness. Through the force of the goodness that has been done, may you experience good health, long life, happiness, and well-being.

The last section of the chant is: "By the power of the Buddha, by the power of the Dhamma, by the power of the Sangha, may the devas protect you by the forces of goodness, and may you live happily."

So it is a very beautiful chant, and it is unfortunate that we still haven't got it together yet in English. They are called *anumodana* chants, and there are a few different ones. *Anumodana* literally means "delighting in the goodness that has been done." So that's the gist of it.

Q: Could you please talk about the difference between awareness and consciousness? Is awareness a conditioned state, the way consciousness is? How can we be aware if not through consciousness?

A: Exactly. You can't really separate out the *khandhas*, the five aggregates of being. You can by using language and concepts, but, in reality, they're tied together, rely on each other, and depend on each other. The difference between awareness and consciousness is that consciousness is the basic function of being able to be aware through the sense doors: eye consciousness, ear consciousness, nose consciousness, tongue consciousness, body consciousness, and mind consciousness. The ability to be conscious of sensory contact—that's a basic function. If you live, exist, and have a body and a mind, then you have a basic function of consciousness.

Awareness is a function of *saṅkhārā*, mental formations. The distinguishing characteristic of saṅkhārā is *cetanā* (volition or intention), so that we are directing the awareness. The ability to direct awareness and bring awareness into being is a function of the application of volition and attention. So we can become skilled in the use of awareness, or we can be forgetful in the use of awareness. This needs to be nurtured, looked after, and developed. Consciousness, receiving sensory contact, is just a basic function.

That's the basic difference. They're both conditioned. We direct awareness in consciousness as well. By becoming increasingly aware of what we are conscious of, we can make clearer decisions and more clearly discern what is actually happening to us.

Q: Would you be willing to share some of your personal journey, including some description of your life before you became a monk?

Why did you choose to become a monk? Could you shed light on how the holy life can help people grow and change?

A: I have a very short life history. I grew up in a podunk little town in Canada and got out of there as soon as I could. I became interested in Buddhism in university in the 1960s. I grew up in the province of Manitoba. The town I grew up in is six-hundred miles north of the US border. There wasn't much Buddhism happening up there then, and there still isn't. Then I went to university in Winnipeg, which is a nice city, but small, in midwestern Canada. So I didn't come into contact with any teachings or teachers.

But I had an interest. I tracked down as many books as I could on Buddhism. And then after finishing university and working long enough to get some money, I headed off traveling. Many people did in those days. I traveled through Europe, the Middle East, and India. I had a vague idea that I would go to Japan to study Buddhism. In those days, the majority of the books you could get on Buddhism were about Zen.

But then I arrived in Thailand. There were all these monasteries around. It looked like it was a Buddhist culture. I was really fascinated, so I stayed on. I went to a few different monasteries and practiced here and there. My introduction to meditation was a solitary, one-month Mahasi Sayadaw retreat. That was how I started to learn to meditate, and I loved it. I wondered, "How do I do more of this?"

It was a bit difficult because they tell you to meditate twenty hours a day and sleep four. And given the instructions, I felt four hours couldn't be real, so I just disregarded that. It just didn't sink in; it wasn't a part of my reality.

I was meditating diligently, as much as I could, and having some very interesting states. Then there was a bit of a plateau after about ten days or two weeks. Then after a couple of days, the teacher asked, "How much are you sleeping?" I said, "Maybe six or seven hours a night." I thought that was pretty good because I could see my sleep dropping. And he chewed me out: "You slacker! You've been cheating. You've built up all this sleep. Two hours a night! That's all you can have. Go back and meditate." So I had lots of interesting experience with meditation.

I went to another monastery and took temporary ordination. It was a city monastery on the outskirts of Bangkok. That's where I started hearing about the forest tradition and Ajahn Chah, and that sounded really attractive to me. After I'd been a monk for only a month, I asked my teacher if I could go up to visit and pay my respects to Ajahn Chah. He said that he had heard about him and that he was a very good monk.

So I left and went to Ajahn Chah's monastery in the early morning. You see monks coming back from almsrounds, winter mists in the fields. It's very ethereal. I came in as everything was quiet and composed and got the opportunity to pay respects to Ajahn Chah. So I bowed and finished my bowing, and he looked at me and said, "If you want to stay here, you have to stay at least five years." So I felt, "Oh, I guess it's not for me."

I stayed for a while and then went off to another monastery that was very quiet. I was putting a lot of effort into practice. Meditation was going very well. I was very diligent in practice. The months were going by, but I just kept thinking of Ajahn Chah all the time. I thought, "Well, five years is five years. I'll go back and give myself to Ajahn Chah." That's thirty-five years ago.

In terms of how the holy life can help people grow and change, especially having been in robes for such a long time and been in monasteries where people come and go, one thing that is clear to me is there is no such thing as the ideal monastic or ideal practitioner. I've seen so many types of people come. Some people stay and some people go. Some people are absolutely inspired and seem so composed, knowledgeable, and clear, and then they disappear in the middle of the night. Other people come, and, despite problem after problem and difficulty after difficulty, they stick with it and they change. That is one of the things that is consistent: if somebody stays with it, change takes place. People really do grow and change.

Q: It has been so helpful to hear stories from your own experience. Could you talk about some of the more challenging moments in your practice and how you worked with them?

A: I've shared a few things, especially in terms of conflicts with others. One of the things that might be useful is dealing with doubt. That is something that we all experience: doubt in ourselves, doubt in the practice. One thing that I have found interesting is that it isn't actually me resolving doubt. It is allowing the practice or Dhamma to work. It's like getting on the bus: it will take us to where its destination is. We don't really need to figure everything out or have it all absolutely clear, but there is a basic foundation of trust in the teachings and practice. We give ourselves to that, the vehicle of the Buddha, Dhamma, and Sangha, and see what the results are.

Those qualities of generosity, virtue, mindfulness, training, and reflection on basic themes are a trustworthy vehicle. Just plug into that, getting into the vehicle and allowing it to carry you. After some time these qualities start to mature and, as you stick with the practice, there is a realization. It isn't as if you had an insight into the doubt and it dissolved, but at some point you say, "I used to have doubt about that. I used to worry about that. That's not there anymore. That's interesting." On reflection, you see that the doubt has unraveled because of the power of the practice and path itself. Confidence in the efficacy of the path and training grows and continues to grow.

Q: What is the Pali word for letting go or relinquishment? Please spell that as well.

A: Well there are a few different words that sometimes get tied into the phrase "letting go." *Nālaṃ abhinivesāya*: all *dhammas* are not to be clung to. Not clinging is, of course, letting go. *Paṭinissagga* directly means relinquishment or letting go. *Vossagga* is relinquishment, particularly around the sense of self—letting go of the sense of self or "I."

This comes up in many suttas in which the Buddha outlines a course of practice. Each step of the practice is accompanied by reflection on impermanence or solitude, and then dispassion and cessation, culminating in relinquishment. The cultivation of *ānāpānasati*, mindfulness of breathing, culminates in reflections on impermanence, cessation, and relinquishment, which are important terms for reflection.

Q: Is this relinquishment, letting go, the opposite of *upādāna*?

A: Yes, it would be the opposite of that clinging.

Q: Is *attavādupādāna* clinging to *sakkāya-diṭṭhi*?

A: There are four different types of upādāna. The last one is *attavādupādāna*, which is the clinging to the belief in self. *Sakkāya-diṭṭhi* is one of the fetters; it is the identification with the body-mind complex. Attavādupādāna is much broader. It would still play itself out in the more refined types of clinging to self and self-conceit. It forms the basis of sakkāya-diṭṭhi but is broader. The difference between attavādupādāna and *diṭṭhupādāna* is that *diṭṭhupādāna* is clinging to views, while attavādupādāna is the clinging to belief in self. It is interesting that the structure of the language is not "clinging to self" because the self is non-existent. Rather, it is the clinging to the belief in self.

Q: Do you think being interested in Buddhism guided you to the contemplative life or would you have become a monk in any tradition? Would you share a bit of your story?

A: Certainly there was a draw to some kind of contemplative life. When I was young, religion didn't draw me, although that is probably a manifestation of stubbornness and contrariness. But something resonated immediately with Buddhism and something drew me to meditation and training the mind. I was looking for ways to do that.

I remember when I was still in university. I was out east and visiting an uncle and aunt of mine. I was already interested in Buddhism, and we were talking and something came up about religion, Buddhism, and meditation. My aunt said that she remembered looking after me when I was a small child—she had asked me what I wanted to be when I grew up, and I said I wanted to be a priest. I remember being very embarrassed. I had another friend traveling with me, and I remember thinking, "Oh, dear." But I can see that something resonated, even if it wasn't conscious. Something was definitely drawing me to some kind of spiritual tradition and training.

Q: Could you say a few more words on posture? For example, I noticed that my body was leaning towards the left, and if I weighted my right hand with intention, this seemed to stop. Is this a correct tactic? In my marital arts training the goal is to relax and make the breathing easier. Is that true of *vipassanā* as well?

A: I haven't addressed posture very much on this retreat; I somehow skipped over it. Posture is a very helpful anchor for awareness: being able to attend to posture, paying attention to a balance of posture and the energy we bring into the posture. It is very helpful in terms of the practice: recognizing where our bodies either slump, lean, or drift. It is helpful for balancing energy within the body-mind complex, but you also start to get an inkling of what's going on in your body-mind.

What is important is relaxing into the posture, and then allowing the breathing to flow quite easily. If you're sitting slumped over, it's very difficult to breathe. The mind tends to get dull; the body will tend to ache. If there is a nice, balanced posture, the body can sit still for longer periods of time.

You can't force the body into sitting still. Sitting straight up, you just get tense, but if you continue to relax, allow the breathing to soften and balance, and let the posture balance the energy, then you find that there is a lightness within the body and mind.

One of the things I try to draw attention to is that whenever you go into a shrine room where there is a Buddha image, you almost always see that it has a very nice posture. It is the archetype of balance and composure.

I remember the very first time that Ajahn Sumedho came back from England. He had gone to England to establish a monastery and had been there for several years. He came back to visit and pay his respects to Ajahn Chah. One of the gifts he brought was a Buddha image that had been sculpted by an English student there. The image was very upright. Ajahn Chah saw it, was quiet for a while, and looked at it from time to time. In the Thai language, the word for "westerner" is *farang*. Finally he said, "It looks like a farang Buddha. It looks very tense."

Q: Could you please explain devas to us? I had an experience yesterday after the Dhamma talk in which I may have seen a group of beings above us, particularly above you. This is not the first experience I've had with perceiving other-worldly beings, but this is the first time new ones communicated to me. They seemed to indicate that they particularly wanted me to be free from anxiety. Today, they also led me to radiate compassion using the phrases from the second stanza of the sublime-abiding chant that we did this afternoon. Once I focused on this a while, they seemed calmer, and I no longer felt their presence. I don't think I'm crazy, but I'm very interested in what the Dhamma says about other-worldly, non-material beings.

A: Unfortunately, I'm one of the last people to talk about any direct experience with this. I don't see other realms or other beings. When I used to live at Wat Nanachat, there was a cremation ground, so there were many ghosts as well as many devas. On more than one occasion, either laypeople or monks good at this would come up to me and say, "Such and such deva in that place and that spirit in that place would like you to dedicate merit and offer blessings." They always had to use an intermediary. I was thick, thick, thick. I don't get it.

My own experience, having lived in Thailand a long time, a place that has a totally different world view, is that other people whom I trusted had these experiences. It certainly seems that they are just another part of reality.

That being said, it can also be a sign of psychosis, so it can be a delicate balance. Once you meet someone who is communicating with other beings in other realms, you might need to call in a psychiatrist or a psychotherapist. So it does call for circumspection, but I have met many people who are very stable and sane, who say there are realms of devas, particularly in a place like this, which is a natural environment. In a place that's protected, there will be many such beings, tree devas, forest devas, and earth devas, and they would particularly be drawn to loving-kindness. It draws a crowd; it feels good. This is a natural phenomenon. I see it as a part of nature.

One of the monks we had visiting us last year, Luang Por Plien, has a very tangible connection with other realms, which came in very useful. Casa Serena at Abhayagiri, the women's residence and place of practice, was offered by someone who had passed away in the house itself. Many of the Thai women who stay there are frightened that there might be ghosts there, so when he came to Abhayagiri he was asked, "Luang Por Plien, please come over to Casa Serena, sit in meditation, and give me the straight scoop. Are there any ghosts here?" We went over and did blessing chants, and he sat and later said, "There are no ghosts here. They were reborn immediately by the force of their goodness. There is nothing but good spirits here." Not having direct experience, being able to rely on Ajahn Plien was very helpful.

Q: What is the difference between meditating on and contemplating or thinking about something? Could you give some examples about someone who would be skillfully meditating on something versus unskillfully doing so? And what does *saṅkhāra* mean?

A: "Meditating" is a generic term. "Contemplating" definitely has the sense of reflection, investigation, and thinking. Meditation can use the thought process, but also, the thought process can be still. We use contemplation and reflection to help the meditation process, either in the sense of bringing up a sense of urgency or bringing up positive states of mind, but in the end, meditation, ideally, turns into a stillness, a silence, a freedom from the thought process.

This doesn't mean that we aren't able to discern anything, but that restless thinking, that compulsion to ruminate, settles, and the mind becomes still and clear. There's a stability and clarity that allows us to see things in a different light, the light of relinquishment, the light of passing away or ceasing, recognizing things coming to cessation, settling.

So, we aren't thinking about it. It's a very direct experience because the mind is still. That would be an example of skillfully meditating. It would be unskillful to obsess on a particular thought process or experience. Even if an experience is one of peace and stillness, one can still obsess on it. There can be assumptions of selfhood or the extrapolation of one's worth and value, like one has a good meditation, so one feels one is a good person. Or one has had a bad meditation, and therefore, one's a bad meditator or bad person. That's unskillful. Recognize that that is just an impermanent experience, arising and ceasing, so there is space around it.

Saṅkhāra probably has one of the longest definitions in the Pali-English dictionary. It is a complicated word and concept, and it's used in different contexts. In a literal sense, it is something that is built, compounded, or created. So in the chant that we do, *sabbe saṅkhārā aniccā* means, "All things of a compounded nature are impermanent." But the phrase is also used in *rūpaṃ aniccaṃ, vedanā aniccā*, and *saññā aniccā*, as well as *saṅkhārā aniccā*. It's used in the context of the khandhas, the aggregates of being. And there is also a specific meaning of *saṅkhāra* that refers to mental states, mental formations, which are the compounded and compounding, volitional aspect of mental activities.

Q: When I think of people with spontaneous, open, and generous hearts, they are full of mettā, *karuṇā*, and muditā but do not seem equanimous. Can upekkhā come naturally, as well as be cultivated?

A: I think it really is more a result of cultivation because it isn't immediately apparent in human experience that equanimity has value. We can see the value in loving-kindness, compassion, (*karuṇā*) and sympathetic joy (the freedom from jealousy), but it isn't immediately apparent what is good about equanimity.

The others are more bound with becoming and all the positive connotations we have associated with a good human being. We don't appreciate the sense of upekkhā, the equanimity, equipoise, and balance, until we start to reflect and investigate and see how difficult it actually is to sustain that: to be present with something, not moved by circumstance, not moved internally with the moods or impressions within the mind.

When we say not moved, it doesn't mean dull, shut down, or closed off, but being completely in tune, very clear, and not being shaken by anything. It takes some time to appreciate that and then recognize that this is going to take some cultivation and work. Of course, when we recognize the benefits of not being dragged into our own internal or external reactivity or the expectations of the world around us, there is tremendous freedom in that quality of equanimity.

As we cultivate and attend to the qualities of mettā, karuṇā, and muditā, as we become more attuned to the sublime nature of these wholesome qualities, then we also start to recognize the nature of the mind, in the sense that our desires are always outstripping our experience. So, you get your latest gadget and it has more memory and it's faster: "I'd like one of those."

We do the same things in spiritual practice. It can torment us, but it is also quite natural. When it's channeled, we can try to put it to skillful use. As we cultivate loving-kindness and compassion, we can think, "Well that's pretty good, but I bet there is something more." Well, in fact, there is. Equanimity is the refinement that allows us to be drawn towards true peace.

Q: What is the difference between *pīti* and sukha?

A: These are qualities that usually arise in meditation as we develop a continuity of awareness and the mind becomes more and more settled, composed, and unified. The description of the first *jhāna*, or stage of absorption, includes *vitakka-vicāra*, or directed thought and evaluation, *pīti*, sukha, and *ekaggatā*, which is unification of mind.

Pīti is usually translated as joy and sukha as happiness. The classic description from the *Visuddhimagga* is a very good illustration of the difference between the two. The image is of a person walking through an area of wilderness with no source of water or shade, so that there is an experience of heat, discomfort, and suffering. As you continue on your journey, you see some people coming. It looks like they are freshly washed. They look refreshed, and their clothes are clean. They say, "Well, just over there, you can see on the horizon an area of forest where there are trees. There is water there. You will be able to bathe and drink and rest as much as you like." The feeling that comes up is a sense of joy.

You continue the journey and arrive at that oasis or forest area. It is cool. It is shaded. There is water there. You are able to bathe, refresh yourself, and drink your fill. The feeling that arises then is sukha or happiness. So the joy is in the expectation and the happiness is in the experience.

So, similarly in practice, as we begin to have a continuity of awareness and attention, the mind becomes more settled and we start to have a joyful energy coming through the body. The feeling of joyful energy that we experience is pīti, which can be experienced in different ways. Sometimes when you are sitting and meditating and the mind is settling, there might be some tingling and a rushing feeling in the body. The breathing is deep and the body is experiencing a sense of joy, but it's not so settled.

With sukha, we continue with that attentiveness and mindfulness, and as the mind is not shaken or distracted by the joy, the happiness becomes much more pervasive throughout the body. The mind and body become relaxed and settled. Feelings of pain and discomfort are completely gone, and there is a feeling of well-being.

So those are the differences between pīti and sukha. Pīti can be a bit exciting. Sometimes you are meditating, reflecting on some aspect of Dhamma, and tears of joy come. It's hard to get peaceful and settled with tears running down your face: you need to blow your nose.

Keep being mindful and it settles into a steadier sukha, happiness, which is very pervasive. Do not try to control or force things at this point. Allow the mind to move into the object of attention. There is a unification of mind.

Pīti and sukha are very helpful tools in practice, but they are also a natural result. People experience them in different ways. If you create an idea or concept of it, you will almost certainly block it off. The most important aspect of practice is mindfulness; that's really the bedrock or bottom line. Keep coming back to the quality of mindful attention and awareness.

The Five Aggregates Affected by Clinging

Because the five aggregates are empty and hollow, we
need to be very careful and attentive around them.

Last night during the question and answer session, there was a question asking about a reference for a sutta that talked about "path and fruit" and the stages of liberation: the path of liberation and the fruit of liberation. So I went back last night and scoured some books. There was also a question the other night about what is fun about being a monk, and I had fun last night.

This sutta is something people may have heard referenced in different places. The Buddha is giving a discourse about the eight wonderful and marvelous qualities of the ocean. One that is well known is that the ocean has but one taste, the taste of salt. And just as the ocean has one taste, the taste of salt, even so this Dhamma and Discipline, which is what the Buddha called his dispensation, has but one taste: the taste of liberation (A 8:19).

The eighth quality is that: "Just as the great ocean is the abode of great beings, so too this Dhamma and Discipline is the abode of great beings: the stream-enterer and the one practicing for the realization of the fruit of stream-entry; the once-returner and the one practicing for the realization of the fruit of once-returning; the non-returner and the one practicing for the fruit of non-returning; the arahant and the one practicing for arahantship. This is the eighth astounding and amazing quality of this Dhamma and Discipline because of which the monks take delight in it." (A 8:19)

As I was poking around, I came across a delightful sutta that I thought I would read this morning, which also concerns the fruits of realization and, in particular, the first access into the realization of stream-entry.

On one occasion the Blessed One was dwelling among the Sakyans at Kapilavattu in the Banyan Tree Park. [That was his hometown.] Then Mahānāma the Sakyan approached the Blessed One, paid homage to him, sat down to one side, and said to the Blessed One:

"Bhante, how does a noble disciple, who has arrived at the fruit and understood the teaching, often dwell?" [That is, the realization of stream-entry.]

"Mahānāma, a noble disciple, who has arrived at the fruit and understood the teaching, often dwells in this way:

(1) "Here, Mahānāma, a noble disciple recollects the Tathāgata thus: 'The Blessed One is an arahant, perfectly enlightened, accomplished in true knowledge and conduct, fortunate, knower of the world, unsurpassed trainer of persons to be tamed, teacher of devas and humans, the Enlightened One, the Blessed One.' When a noble disciple recognizes the Tathāgata thus, on that occasion his mind is not obsessed with lust, hatred or delusion; on that occasion his mind is simply straight, based on the Tathāgata. A noble disciple whose mind is straight gains inspiration in the meaning, gains inspiration in the Dhamma, gains joy connected with the Dhamma. When he is joyful, rapture arises. For one with a rapturous mind, the body becomes tranquil. One tranquil in body feels pleasure. For one feeling pleasure, the mind becomes concentrated. This is called a noble disciple who dwells in balance amid an unbalanced population, who dwells unafflicted amid an afflicted population. As one who has entered upon the stream of the Dhamma, he develops recollection of the Buddha.

(2) "Again, Mahānāma, a noble disciple recollects the Dhamma thus: 'The Dhamma is well expounded by the Blessed One, directly visible, immediate, inviting one to come and see, applicable, to be personally experienced by the wise.' When a noble disciple recollects the Dhamma, on that occasion his mind is not obsessed by lust, hatred, and delusion; on that occasion his mind is simply straight, based on the Dhamma . . . This is called a noble disciple

who dwells in balance amid an unbalanced population, who dwells unafflicted amid an afflicted population. As one who has entered upon the stream of the Dhamma, he develops recollection of the Dhamma.

(3) "Again, Mahānāma, a noble disciple recollects the Sangha thus: 'The Sangha of the Blessed One's disciples is practicing the good way, practicing the straight way, practicing the true way, practicing the proper way; that is, the four pairs of persons, the eight types of individuals—this Sangha of the Blessed One's disciples is worthy of gifts, worthy of hospitality, worthy of offerings, worthy of reverential salutation, the unsurpassed field of merit for the world.' When a noble disciple recollects the Sangha, on that occasion his mind is not obsessed by lust, hatred, and delusion; on that occasion his mind is simply straight, based on the Sangha . . . This is called a noble disciple who dwells in balance amid an unbalanced population, who dwells unafflicted amid an afflicted population. As one who has entered upon the stream of the Dhamma, he develops recollection of the Sangha.

(4) "Again, Mahānāma, a noble disciple recollects his own virtuous behavior as unbroken, flawless, unblemished, unblotched, freeing, praised by the wise, ungrasped, leading to concentration. When a noble disciple recollects his virtuous behavior, on that occasion his mind is not obsessed by lust, hatred, and delusion; on that occasion his mind is simply straight, based on virtuous behavior . . . This is called a noble disciple who dwells in balance amid an unbalanced population, who dwells unafflicted amid an afflicted population. As one who has entered the stream of the Dhamma, he develops recollection of virtuous behavior.

(5) "Again, Mahānāma, a noble disciple recollects his own generosity thus: 'It is truly my good fortune and gain that in a population obsessed by the stain of miserliness, I dwell at home with a mind devoid of the stain of miserliness, freely generous, openhanded, delighting in relinquishment, devoted to charity, delighting in giving and sharing.' When a noble disciple recollects his own generosity, on that occasion his mind is not obsessed by lust, hatred, and delusion; on that occasion his mind is simply straight, based on generosity . . . This is called a noble disciple who dwells in balance amid an unbalanced population, who dwells unafflicted

amid an afflicted population. As one who has entered the stream of the Dhamma, he develops recollection of generosity.

"Again, Mahānāma, a noble disciple recollects the deities thus: 'There are devas [ruled by] the four great kings, Tāvatiṃsa devas, Yāma devas, Tusita devas, devas who delight in creation, devas who control what is created by others, devas of Brahmā's company, and devas still higher than these. There exists in me too such faith as those deities possessed because of which, when they passed away here, they were born there. There is found in me such virtuous behavior . . . such learning . . . such generosity . . . such wisdom as those deities possessed because of which, when they passed away from here, they were reborn there.' When a noble disciple recollects the faith, virtuous behavior, learning, generosity, and wisdom in himself and in those deities, on that occasion his mind is not obsessed by lust, hatred, and delusion; on that occasion his mind is simply straight, based on the deities. A noble disciple whose mind is straight gains inspiration in the meaning, gains inspiration in the Dhamma, gains joy connected with the Dhamma. When he is joyful, rapture arises. For one with a rapturous mind, the body becomes tranquil. One tranquil in body feels pleasure. For one feeling pleasure, the mind becomes concentrated. This is called a noble disciple who dwells in balance amid an unbalanced population, who dwells unafflicted amid an afflicted population. As one who has entered the stream of the Dhamma, he develops recollection of the deities.

"Mahānāma, a noble disciple, who has arrived at the fruit and understood the teaching, often dwells in just this way."

(A 6:10)

One of the things that I like to point out is that, particularly in terms of meditation, there are different recollections such as these to which we can direct our attention and then there is gladness connected with the Dhamma, arising on account of that. When there is gladness, then rapture arises. When one is uplifted in rapture, the body becomes calm. One who is calm in body feels happy. For one who is happy, the mind becomes concentrated.

That is usually backwards from how we approach our meditation. "When I get my *samādhi*, then I'm going to be happy." All the effort is put into trying to get the mind to comply with the wish to be still and concentrated. Rather, we should pay attention to those qualities that bring a sense of well-being, gladness, calming, and happiness. Concentration arises out of that. That is a way of establishing well-being, allowing the mind to settle from there.

On a certain level, the gladness connected to the Dhamma is also from seeing more clearly how these different things fit together. What is the obstruction to cultivating loving-kindness? Almost invariably, it will be the sense of self that impinges on consciousness, and not just impinges on consciousness, but looms. Reflect that the nature of how we construct a sense of self is a burden and reflect on that in terms of Dhamma, with respect to the five *khandhas*.

When we do the morning chanting, we go through all of the different aspects of suffering. Then the chant ties it all up, saying, "In brief, the five focuses of the grasping mind are dukkha." This is a recognition that these *pañcupādāna-kkhandhā* (the aggregates of being) are affected by grasping, clinging, and attachment. The identification with body, feeling, perception, mental formations, and consciousness—the habit of attachment and clinging—is what is intrinsically bound up with suffering, dissatisfaction, and discontent, and then spills out into all of the various forms of afflicted emotional states. So investigate those five aggregates of being.

There is a discourse (S 22:100) in which the Buddha gives an image of a dog being tied to a post. Whether that dog lies down, stands up, sits, or walks, it is tied to that post. And the Buddha says as long as we are bound up and tied to those five khandhas—identification with the body, feelings, perceptions, mental formations, and consciousness—then in the same way, whether we walk, stand, sit, or lie down, we're bound with suffering, discontent, and dissatisfaction: dukkha.

That whole process of identification with body, feelings, perceptions, mental formations, and consciousness—"this is mine, this is what I am, this is my self"—is inevitably productive of suffering. It's inherent. It's intrinsic. It can't be any other way.

So recognize how clinging, attachment, and identification keep coalescing and forming, establishing themselves. And then recognize that there is an opportunity of non-clinging, non-attachment: "How do I do that? How do I not cling to everything I conceive of as my self?"

If you have ever gone on a long hike with too much stuff, when you put that pack on, you think, "It's a bit heavy, but it's okay." But you keep walking and the pack gets heavier and heavier. And you say, "Well, I shouldn't have taken this much stuff, but maybe I'll need it." You keep carrying it and carrying it, and you think, "I've got to get rid of some of this stuff." You let it go because you can't carry it any longer.

It's the same thing with attachment and clinging when you realize that this is a burden and you don't really want to carry it any longer. You're willing to put it down, get rid of it, drop it. That's the good news. The bad news is we usually have to wait until we are really willing to put it down.

The Buddha has us reflect on and investigate these aspects of the khandhas and their emptiness, their ephemeral nature. The Buddha once offered a discourse (S 22:95) when he was by a river. As often happens, there was some foam on the river, and the Buddha used that as an example.

"See that foam on the river? That foam is just like our bodies. That foam is insubstantial, empty, and hollow. In the same way our bodies are just like that." If we reflect on the nature of the body, it seems substantial. As we age and get sick, we see that there is really not much here. All of the different cells and other bodily constituents are really insubstantial.

The same is true with feeling. In Asia, the monsoon season brings big, fat, heavy raindrops. When the rain comes down, little bubbles come up. Feeling is like those bubbles. A little bubble forms and it bursts. Another little bubble forms and it bursts. That's exactly like feeling.

It's good to clarify that "feeling" refers specifically to pleasant, painful, and neutral feeling. It's a basic quality of experience, of sensation—not feelings in terms of emotions. It's the basic tone of any kind of contact: pleasant, painful, or neutral. Sights, sounds, smells, taste, touch, and mind objects: there's always an associated feeling tone. Because those experiences are arising and ceasing, the feeling tone is arising and ceasing. They are little bubbles arising and popping, arising and popping. We tend to react and respond to them with our preferences, so we end up layering that very simple feeling tone with our likes and dislikes, wanting and not wanting. But if we reflect, there is just a basic feeling, arising and ceasing.

The Buddha compares perception to a mirage, like in the hot season in India or in America out on the plains. I guess the Central Valley would get enough heat to form a mirage, images that shimmer in the distance. It looks like something, and then when you get closer, it's not that.

Perception is also bound up with memory, giving meaning to things, which we build through memory: how we value and give importance to things, how we hold them through the nature of perception. There's not really a thinking process going on with that. We perceive something in a certain way, affected by memory and how we have perceived it over time as well.

Ajahn Amaro recently gave a talk in which he related an experience he had when he was in England as a young monk. He did a long walk from our monastery in the south of England to a branch monastery up near the Scottish border. He had completed his fifth Rains Retreat, which is a time when monks have the opportunity to spread their wings a bit. He wanted to try a walk, as a monk, in England and went with a layman who would be able to help out if necessary. This was the first time in our community that anyone had tried a long walk as an alms mendicant in the West, and it took them several months.

This last spring the two of them got together and revisited the walk. They didn't do the whole thing. They did parts of it for the 25th anniversary of their quite historic walk.

The really interesting thing was that virtually every place they went back to, something had been moved. A hill had moved; a house had moved. It had been so vivid in his memory and he had told the story so many times, but when he actually went back, it wasn't how he had remembered it or had related it to people. It was different.

Saññā aniccā: perception is impermanent. Perception is not a mechanical function that is solid. It's the *upādāna-kkhandha* (the aggregate of being affected by attachment and clinging). Clinging arises out of like or dislike, or some kind of delusion. It doesn't have to be gross. We pick up on gross things, but it is the subtle things that are really believable. Then we build on them and they become our reality.

That is our unfortunate circumstance as human beings. We live in a world that we have created and that is a function of our wishes. The unacknowledged agenda is, "Boy, if I could just build the world the way I wanted it! Wow, that would be great!" But the reality of the noble truth of suffering is that we then have to live in that world.

Perception is one of the fundamental things we build the world out of: our identification with self—*my* position, *my* preference, *my* idea, *my* ideal, *my* fear. It's not really thought through. It's a much deeper stratum of the mind than thinking and planning, and it overlays everything. Reflect on the nature of these aggregates of being. Reflect on the nature of perception. Perception is like a mirage, although that may not be the way we naturally conceive it.

The Buddha compared the mental formations to a banana tree. A person goes into the forest looking for hardwood and cuts down a plantain tree, a banana tree. If anyone has seen a banana tree, it's layer after layer of leaves. There is no core to it. It seems solid: six inches, eight inches, twelve inches around. But as we take each layer off, we can peel it all back and there is nothing there. There's just another leaf inside.

So the nature of mental formations, thought processes, is that there are just these layers but no solid core. It is absurd to consider, "What is my one true thought?" But this doesn't mean that we can't use thoughts, emotions, and planning, all of which take place within mental formations. Mental formations can be related to ill will, aversion, desire, attachment, fear, or anxiety. Mindfulness is also a mental formation. Wisdom, loving-kindness, compassion, and equanimity are all mental formations, but they have a usefulness and skill to them, a beneficial result.

So it's not, "Oh, mental formations are a banana tree. I'm done with that." No. We really have to know how to use, understand, and skillfully apply the thought processes and not be trapped or caught by them. It's when we see this more clearly that we develop a certain wariness toward the thought processes.

We have been using thoughts of mettā as a practice. We can see these wholesome mental formations starting to gain momentum over irritation, aversion, or a negative viewpoint that has arisen. We see that if we let that go—"I know where this is going, I know where this will end"—we'll turn our attention to loving-kindness. We'll turn our attention to well-wishing. We can counter the negative impulses. By seeing mental formations as empty and hollow, we won't just push them away. Because they are empty and hollow, we need to be very careful and attentive around them.

The Buddha has us reflect on consciousness. He compares it to a magician or conjurer's trick. In India, in the marketplace or on the street corner, there can be a magician or conjurer, a person doing magic tricks. There is a small crowd around him and he is making a little money with it. Today, the same scene is still going on, 2,500 years later. If we understand the nature of the conjurer's trick, the mechanics behind it, there's not the same excitement or fascination. We're not as willing to lay money down to see the trick again.

The nature of consciousness is very similar. We take these disparate experiences—contact with the senses—and form them into an experience. "Yeah, he really said that." We have formed the consciousness of that experience really happening, and we remember it a certain way, but actually, there is an agenda behind consciousness as well. We have to recognize the hook buried in it.

We will never be free of the five khandhas, the five aggregates of being. But we can be free from being affected by clinging to the aggregates, and that is the most important part because we do need to rely on those five aggregates of being. That's how we live; that's how we accomplish things.

That's how the Buddha was able to teach—with the five khandhas. If he had said, "Well, that's it for the five khandhas," and had done nothing, then we would be in a bind. After the Buddha's enlightenment, he spent forty-five years carrying the khandhas around and teaching, establishing a dispensation that has lasted to this day.

This reflection on the khandhas is a really important part of understanding the nature of self and attachment to self, the nature of clinging, and then the nature of relinquishment, letting go. As we are able to attend to letting go, part of the response is the sense of loving-kindness. It is a natural response of seeing Dhamma, seeing things the way they are, that kindness and compassion arise, the sense of not being trapped by the particular reactions that come up.

I remember Ajahn Jumnien saying that whenever anybody comes to him saying, "Well, I've attained it. I've had stream-entry now. No more rebirth in the lower realms for me. I'm really pleased with my practice," he will usually find the occasion to say, "Well, you know so-and-so has been saying this about you. They have been saying you're like this and like that." Then he would see what sort of response there was because if there is anger, thinking, "How could they say that?" then the person is not a stream-enterer.

Here, once again, that holding on to identity is one of the hallmarks of worldly existence. The relinquishment of that identification process is one of the fetters that is dropped as one enters the stream of Dhamma.

Ajahn Chah did something similar to someone who came to him. He was saying how well his practice was growing, that he was practicing really diligently and had had a breakthrough and was quite confident now that it was clear sailing to arahantship. Ajahn Chah just grunted and said, "That's better than being a dog." Especially in Thai, when you compare somebody to being a dog, it's *bad*. That person got extremely upset. Ajahn couldn't help but relate this by saying, "So much for the stream-enterer."

So loving-kindness, that inclination to well-wishing, is an integral part of the Dhamma. As we cultivate loving-kindness, it is not something that is separate from practicing Dhamma, reflecting on Dhamma. They are woven together and support each other. We cultivate and bring loving-kindness into being not only to help establish wholesome states of consciousness and calm states of abiding. It also lays a foundation for insight because it is a helpful tool for creating a stability and brightness of mind that allows us to see the Dhamma. We reflect on and investigate Dhamma but also see that this is a result. They work together and are interwoven. So giving attention to these qualities is something that allows us to gain inspiration and confidence in the Dhamma.

Sutta Readings

Even something as sublime as loving-kindness is
impermanent. Seeing its changing nature can be
a basis for investigation and penetration.

This afternoon, I thought I'd take the opportunity to do some sutta readings about loving-kindness and give people the real scoop—I've rambled on long enough. There are some sutta readings that are interesting in that they are not so familiar to people or take something familiar and cast it in a new light. Then there are some that are daily-life applications of loving-kindness.

The first one I thought I would read is one I have mentioned. It's an occasion when the Buddha goes to visit three monks, one of whom is the Venerable Anuruddha, who was a very accomplished monk and also the Buddha's cousin.

The Buddha was departing from a situation not mentioned in the sutta. A particular monastic community was in disharmony. Actually, there was a schism happening in the sangha. The Buddha tried to intervene, and they encouraged the Blessed One to live in peace: "We'll sort this out," which meant, "We are going to go at it tooth and nail. Please don't get in our way." He gave up on them, went off on his own, and came across three monks who were living in a woodland area. The Buddha sat down, and the monks paid their respects to him.

"I hope, Anuruddha, that you are all living in concord, with mutual appreciation, without disputing, blending like milk and water, viewing each other with kindly eyes." "Surely, venerable sir, we are living in concord, with mutual appreciation, without disputing, blending like milk and water, viewing each other with kindly eyes." "But, Anuruddha, how do you live thus?" "Venerable sir, as to that, I think thus: 'It is a gain for me, it is a great gain for me, that I am living with such companions in the holy life.' I maintain bodily acts of loving-kindness towards those venerable ones both openly and privately; I maintain verbal acts of loving-kindness towards them both openly and privately; I maintain mental acts of loving-kindness towards them both openly and privately. I consider: 'Why should I not set aside what I wish to do and do what these venerable ones wish to do?' Then I set aside what I wish to do and do what these venerable ones wish to do. We are different in body, venerable sir, but one in mind." The venerable Nandiya and the venerable Kimbila each spoke likewise, adding: "That is how, venerable sir, we are living in concord, with mutual appreciation, without disputing, blending like milk and water, viewing each other with kindly eyes."

(M 128)

That's a delightful description of what is possible in the human realm. There is another discourse in which the Buddha is trying to convince the monks in Kosambi, the monks referred to in the previous discourse, who had been disputing and creating conflict. He admonishes them and then he outlines a more appropriate, skillful way to live together.

"So, bhikkhus, when you take to quarreling and brawling and are deep in disputes, stabbing each other with verbal daggers, on that occasion you do not maintain acts of loving-kindness by body, speech, and mind in public and in private to your companions in the holy life.

"Misguided men, what can you possibly know, what can you see, that you take to quarreling and brawling and are deep in disputes, stabbing each other with verbal daggers? That you can neither convince each other nor be convinced by others, that you can neither persuade each other nor be persuaded by others?

Misguided men, that will lead to your harm and suffering for a long time." Then the Blessed One addressed the bhikkhus thus: "Bhikkhus, there are these six principles of cordiality that create love and respect and conduce to cohesion, to non-dispute, to concord, and to unity. What are the six?

[1] "Here a bhikkhu maintains bodily acts of loving-kindness both in public and in private towards his companions in the holy life. This is a principle of cordiality that creates love and respect, and conduces to cohesion, to non-dispute, to concord, and to unity.

[2] "Again, a bhikkhu maintains verbal acts of loving-kindness both in public and in private towards his companions in the holy life. This too is a principle of cordiality that creates love and respect, and conduces to . . . unity.

[3] "Again, a bhikkhu maintains mental acts of loving-kindness both in public and in private towards his companions in the holy life. This too is a principle of cordiality that creates love and respect, and conduces to . . . unity.

[4] "Again, a bhikkhu uses things in common with his virtuous companions in the holy life; without making reservations, he shares with them any gain of a kind that accords with the Dhamma and has been obtained in a way that accords with the Dhamma, including even the mere contents of his alms-bowl. This too is a principle of cordiality that creates love and respect, and conduces to . . . unity.

[5] "Again, a bhikkhu dwells both in public and in private possessing in common with his companions in the holy life those virtues that are unbroken, untorn, unblotched, unmottled, liberating, commended by the wise, not misapprehended, and conducive to concentration. This too is a principle of cordiality that creates love and respect, and conduces to . . . unity.

[6] "Again, a bhikkhu dwells both in public and in private possessing in common with his companions in the holy life that view that is noble and emancipating, and leads one who practices in accordance with it to the complete destruction of suffering. This too is a principle of cordiality that creates love and respect, and conduces to cohesion, to non-dispute, to concord, and to unity."

(M 48)

The six qualities of creating concord and living together come up in different places in the suttas: loving-kindness in acts, speech, and thought; sharing with generosity; common virtue and common view. There is also the stock phrase "virtues that are unbroken, untorn, unblotched, unmottled, liberating, commended by the wise, not misapprehended, and conducive to concentration."

These virtues are also talked about as a distinguishing characteristic of one who has entered the stream of Dhamma: a stream-enterer. It is interesting how the Buddha most often describes the stream-enterer not by their dazzling meditations or astute wisdom, but by their qualities of faith in Buddha, Dhamma, and Sangha, and well-established virtue. Such virtue is not misapprehended, not clung to, not attached to. It is commended by the wise and conducive to concentration.

Virtue is settling. There is composure involved. Virtue is not "keeping you in line," but allowing you to be established in a quality of non-remorse and well-being, so that you can concentrate easily. It is a factor of our development of meditation.

This next sutta reading also comes from *The Middle-Length Discourses*. It's a very famous sutta, *The Simile of the Saw*.

There is a buildup to the simile. The incident that gave rise to the teaching is that one of the bhikkhus was in conflict with the other bhikkhus and was not taking admonishment very well. The circumstance came to the attention of the Buddha, so he called the monk to him and gave a teaching. He took the occasion to teach all of the monks who were present, a situation that often happens, not just in the Buddha's time. I do it all the time: a circumstance comes up and it is a great occasion to be used as an example of application of Dhamma within the community.

"So too, bhikkhus, some bhikkhu is extremely gentle, extremely kind, extremely peaceful, so long as disagreeable courses of speech do not touch him. But it is when disagreeable courses of speech touch him that it can be understood whether that bhikkhu is really kind, gentle, and peaceful. I do not call a bhikkhu easy to admonish who is easy to admonish and makes himself easy to admonish only for the sake of getting robes, almsfood, a resting place, and medicinal requisites. Why is that? Because that bhikkhu is not easy to admonish nor makes himself easy to admonish when he gets no robes, almsfood, resting place, and medicinal requisites. But when a bhikkhu is easy to admonish and makes himself easy to admonish because he honors, respects, and reveres the Dhamma, him I call easy to admonish. Therefore, bhikkhus, you should train thus: 'We shall be easy to admonish and make ourselves easy to admonish because we honor, respect, and revere the Dhamma.' That is how you should train, bhikkhus.

"Bhikkhus, there are these five courses of speech that others use when they address you: their speech may be timely or untimely, true or untrue, gentle or harsh, connected with good or with harm, spoken with a mind of loving-kindness or with inner hate . . . Herein, bhikkhus, [regardless of how someone speaks] you should train thus: 'Our minds will remain unaffected, and we shall utter no evil words; we shall abide compassionate for their welfare, with a mind of loving-kindness, without inner hate. We shall abide pervading that person with a mind imbued with loving-kindness, and starting with him, we shall abide pervading the all-encompassing world with a mind imbued with loving-kindness, abundant, exalted, immeasurable, without hostility and without ill will.' That is how you should train, bhikkhus.

"Bhikkhus, suppose a man came with a hoe and a basket and said: 'I shall make this great earth to be without earth.' He would dig here and there, strew the soil here and there, spit here and there, and urinate here and there, saying: 'Be without earth, be without earth!' What do you think, bhikkhus? Could that man make this great earth to be without earth?"—"No, venerable sir." "Why is that? Because this great earth is deep and immeasurable; it is not easy to make it be without earth. Eventually the man would reap only weariness and disappointment.

"So too, bhikkhus, there are these five courses of speech . . . Herein, bhikkhus, you should train thus: 'Our minds will remain unaffected . . . and starting with him, we shall abide pervading the all-encompassing world with a mind similar to the earth, abundant, exalted, immeasurable, without hostility and without ill will.' That is how you should train, bhikkhus.

"Bhikkhus, suppose a man came with crimson, turmeric, indigo, or carmine and said: 'I shall draw pictures and make pictures appear on empty space.' What do you think, bhikkhus? Could that man draw pictures and make pictures appear on empty space?"—"No, venerable sir." "Why is that? Because empty space is formless and non-manifestive; it is not easy to draw pictures there or make pictures appear there. Eventually the man would reap only weariness and disappointment.

"So too, bhikkhus, there are these five courses of speech . . . Herein, bhikkhus, you should train thus: 'Our minds will remain unaffected . . . and starting with him, we shall abide pervading the all-encompassing world with a mind similar to empty space, abundant, exalted, immeasurable, without hostility and without ill will.' That is how you should train, bhikkhus.

"Bhikkhus, suppose a man came with a blazing grass-torch and said: 'I shall heat up and burn away the river Ganges with this blazing grass-torch.' What do you think, bhikkhus? Could that man heat up and burn away the river Ganges with that blazing grass-torch?"—"No, venerable sir." "Why is that? Because the river Ganges is deep and immense; it is not easy to heat it up or burn it away with a blazing grass-torch. Eventually the man would reap only weariness and disappointment.

"So too, bhikkhus, there are these five courses of speech . . . Herein, bhikkhus, you should train thus: 'Our minds will remain unaffected . . . and starting with him, we shall abide pervading the all-encompassing world with a mind similar to the river Ganges, abundant, exalted, immeasurable, without hostility and without ill will.' That is how you should train, bhikkhus.

"Bhikkhus, suppose there were a catskin bag that was rubbed, well rubbed, thoroughly well rubbed, soft, silky, rid of rustling, rid of crackling, and a man came with a stick or a potsherd and said: 'There is this catskin bag that is rubbed . . . rid of rustling, rid of crackling. I shall make it rustle and crackle.' What do you think, bhikkhus? Could that man make it rustle or crackle with the stick or the potsherd?"—"No, venerable sir." "Why is that? Because that catskin bag being rubbed . . . rid of rustling, rid of crackling, it is not easy to make it rustle or crackle with the stick or the potsherd. Eventually the man would reap only weariness and disappointment.

"So too, bhikkhus, there are these five courses of speech that others may use when they address you: their speech may be timely or untimely, true or untrue, gentle or harsh, connected with good or with harm, spoken with a mind of loving-kindness or with inner hate ... Herein, bhikkhus, [regardless of how someone speaks] you should train thus: 'Our minds will remain unaffected, and we will utter no evil words; we shall abide compassionate for their welfare, with a mind of loving-kindness, without inner hate. We shall abide pervading that person with a mind imbued with loving-kindness; and starting with him, we shall abide pervading the all-encompassing world with a mind similar to a catskin bag, abundant, exalted, immeasurable, without hostility and without ill will.' That is how you should train, bhikkhus.

"Bhikkhus, even if bandits were to sever you savagely limb by limb with a two-handled saw, he who gave rise to a mind of hate towards them would not be carrying out my teaching. Herein, bhikkhus, you should train thus: 'Our minds will remain unaffected, and we shall utter no evil words; we shall abide compassionate for their welfare, with a mind of loving-kindness, without inner hate. We shall abide pervading them with a mind imbued with loving-kindness; and starting with them, we shall abide pervading the all-encompassing world with a mind imbued with loving-kindness, abundant, exalted, immeasurable, without hostility and without ill will.' That is how you should train, bhikkhus.

"Bhikkhus, if you keep this advice on the simile of the saw constantly in mind, do you see any course of speech, trivial or gross, that you could not endure?"—"No, venerable sir."—"Therefore, bhikkhus, you should keep this advice on the simile of the saw constantly in mind. That will lead to your welfare and happiness for a long time."

That is what the Blessed One said. The bhikkhus were satisfied and delighted in the Blessed One's words.

(M 21)

This sets the bar pretty high, doesn't it? You think, "How is it possible when someone is attacking you not to give rise to any anger or ill will?" It's possible if you step back and look at it from a perspective of an abundant heart of loving-kindness and with a conviction in the Dhamma, knowing that because all beings are the owners of their actions, heirs of the actions, born of their actions, and related to their actions, those causes will result in rebirth in a particular way. The result of anger, ill will, or any kind of violence is an unfortunate rebirth. Being well-established in loving-kindness is a cause that produces a result in exceedingly fortunate circumstances. In the long run, it is worth training oneself so the option isn't just aversion, ill will, or irritation.

So those were some suttas in the application of loving-kindness in day-to-day life. There is also an interesting discourse on the application of loving-kindness as a basis for insight. It's a discourse by Ānanda. Ānanda actually defines a number of bases for insight in the jhānas, the four brahmavihāras, and the three formless attainments, but I'll just mention how he describes loving-kindness.

"Again, a bhikkhu abides pervading one quarter with a mind imbued with loving-kindness, likewise the second, likewise the third, likewise the fourth; so above and below, around, and everywhere, and to all as to himself, he abides pervading the all-encompassing world with a mind imbued with loving-kindness, abundant, exalted, immeasurable, without hostility and without ill will. He considers this and understands it thus: 'This deliverance of mind through loving-kindness is conditioned and volitionally produced. But whatever is conditioned and volitionally produced is impermanent, subject to cessation.' If he is steady in that, he attains the destruction of the taints. But if he does not attain the destruction of the taints, then because of that desire for the Dhamma, that delight in the Dhamma, with the destruction of the five lower fetters he becomes one due to appear spontaneously [in the Pure Abodes] and there attain final nibbāna without ever returning from that world.

"This too is one thing proclaimed by the Blessed One . . . wherein if a bhikkhu abides diligent, ardent, and resolute, his unliberated mind comes to be liberated, his undestroyed taints come to be destroyed, and he attains the supreme security from bondage that he had not attained before."

(M 52)

Even something as sublime as loving-kindness is impermanent. Seeing its changing nature can be a basis for investigation and penetration.

I'll do a few readings from *The Numerical Discourses*, the *Aṅguttara Nikāya*. This is addressed to monks but applies to everybody.

"Monks, if for just the time of a finger-snap, a monk produces a thought of loving-kindness, develops it, gives attention to it, such a one is rightly called a monk. Not in vain does he meditate. He acts in accordance with the Master's teaching, he follows his advice, and eats deservingly the country's alms-food. How much more so if he cultivates it."

(A 1:53)

So what we have been doing is not to be sniffed at. The next sutta is one that everyone knows, the *Kālāma Sutta,* but almost never when the *Kālāma Sutta* is quoted does loving-kindness get any mention. So I thought I'd read the complete discourse.

I have heard that on one occasion the Blessed One, on a wandering tour among the Kosalans with a large community of monks, arrived at Kesaputta, a town of the Kālāmas. The Kālāmas of Kesaputta heard it said, "Gotama the contemplative—the son of the Sakyans, having gone forth from the Sakyan clan—has arrived at Kesaputta. And of that Master Gotama this fine reputation has spread: 'He is indeed a Blessed One, worthy, and rightly self-awakened, consummate in knowledge and conduct, well-gone, a knower of the cosmos, an unexcelled trainer of those persons ready to be tamed, teacher of human and divine beings, awakened, blessed. He has made known—having realized it through direct knowledge—this world with its devas, maras, and brahmas, its generations with their contemplatives and brahmans, their rulers and common people; has explained the Dhamma admirable in the beginning, admirable in the middle, admirable in the end; has expounded the holy life both in its particulars and in its essence, entirely perfect, surpassingly pure. It is good to see such a worthy one.'"

So the Kālāmas of Kesaputta went to the Blessed One. On arrival, some of them bowed down to him and sat to one side. Some of them exchanged courteous greetings with him and, after an exchange of friendly greetings and courtesies, sat to one side. Some of them sat to one side having saluted him with their hands palm-to-palm over their hearts. Some of them sat to one side having announced their name and clan. Some of them sat to one side in silence.

As they sat there, the Kālāmas of Kesaputta said to the Blessed One, "Lord, there are some brahmans and contemplatives who come to Kesaputta. They expound and glorify their own doctrines, but as for the doctrines of others, they deprecate them, revile them, show contempt for them, and disparage them. And then other brahmans and contemplatives come to Kesaputta. They expound and glorify their own doctrines, but as for the doctrines of others, they deprecate them, revile them, show contempt for them, and disparage them. They leave us absolutely uncertain and in doubt: Which of these venerable brahmans and contemplatives are speaking the truth, and which ones are lying?"

"Of course you are uncertain, Kālāmas. Of course you are in doubt. When there are reasons for doubt, uncertainty is born. So in this case, Kālāmas, don't go by reports, by legends, by traditions, by scripture, by logical conjecture, by inference, by analogies, by agreement through pondering views, by probability, or by the thought, 'This contemplative is our teacher.' When you know for yourselves that, 'These qualities are unskillful; these qualities are blameworthy; these qualities are criticized by the wise; these qualities, when adopted and carried out, lead to harm and to suffering'—then you should abandon them.

"What do you think, Kālāmas? When greed arises in a person, does it arise for welfare or for harm?"

"For harm, lord."

"And this greedy person, overcome by greed, his mind possessed by greed, kills living beings, takes what is not given, goes after another person's wife, tells lies, and induces others to do likewise, all of which is for long-term harm and suffering."

"Yes, lord."

"Now, what do you think, Kālāmas? When aversion arises in a person, does it arise for welfare or for harm?"

"For harm, lord."

"And this aversive person, overcome by aversion, his mind possessed by aversion, kills living beings, takes what is not given, goes after another person's wife, tells lies, and induces others to do likewise, all of which is for long-term harm and suffering."

"Yes, lord."

"Now, what do you think, Kālāmas? When delusion arises in a person, does it arise for welfare or for harm?"

"For harm, lord."

"And this deluded person, overcome by delusion, his mind possessed by delusion, kills living beings, takes what is not given, goes after another person's wife, tells lies, and induces others to do likewise, all of which is for long-term harm and suffering."

"Yes, lord."

"So what do you think, Kālāmas: Are these qualities skillful or unskillful?"

"Unskillful, lord."

"Blameworthy or blameless?"

"Blameworthy, lord."

"Criticized by the wise or praised by the wise?"

"Criticized by the wise, lord."

"When adopted and carried out, do they lead to harm and to suffering, or not?"

"When adopted and carried out, they lead to harm and to suffering. That is how it appears to us."

"So, as I said, Kālāmas: 'Don't go by reports, by legends, by traditions, by scripture, by logical conjecture, by inference, by analogies, by agreement through pondering views, by probability, or by the thought, "This contemplative is our teacher." When you know for yourselves that, "These qualities are unskillful; these qualities are blameworthy; these qualities are criticized by the wise; these qualities, when adopted and carried out, lead to harm and to suffering"—then you should abandon them.' Thus was it said. And in reference to this was it said.

"Now, Kālāmas, don't go by reports, by legends, by traditions, by scripture, by logical conjecture, by inference, by analogies, by agreement through pondering views, by probability, or by the thought, 'This contemplative is our teacher.' When you know for yourselves that, 'These qualities are skillful; these qualities are blameless; these qualities are praised by the wise; these qualities, when adopted and carried out, lead to welfare and to happiness'—then you should enter and remain in them.

"What do you think, Kālāmas? When lack of greed arises in a person, does it arise for welfare or for harm?"

"For welfare, lord."

"And this ungreedy person, not overcome by greed, his mind not possessed by greed, doesn't kill living beings, take what is not given, go after another person's wife, tell lies, or induce others to do likewise, all of which is for long-term welfare and happiness."

"Yes, lord."

"What do you think, Kālāmas? When lack of aversion arises in a person, does it arise for welfare or for harm?"

"For welfare, lord."

"And this unaversive person, not overcome by aversion, his mind not possessed by aversion, doesn't kill living beings, take what is not given, go after another person's wife, tell lies, or induce others to do likewise, all of which is for long-term welfare and happiness."

"Yes, lord."

"What do you think, Kālāmas? When lack of delusion arises in a person, does it arise for welfare or for harm?"

"For welfare, lord."

"And this undeluded person, not overcome by delusion, his mind not possessed by delusion, doesn't kill living beings, take what is not given, go after another person's wife, tell lies, or induce others to do likewise, all of which is for long-term welfare and happiness."

"Yes, lord."

"So what do you think, Kālāmas: Are these qualities skillful or unskillful?"

"Skillful, lord."

"Blameworthy or blameless?"

"Blameless, lord."

"Criticized by the wise or praised by the wise?"

"Praised by the wise, lord."

"When adopted and carried out, do they lead to welfare and to happiness, or not?"

"When adopted and carried out, they lead to welfare and to happiness. That is how it appears to us."

"So, as I said, Kālāmas: 'Don't go by reports, by legends, by traditions, by scripture, by logical conjecture, by inference, by analogies, by agreement through pondering views, by probability, or by the thought, "This contemplative is our teacher." When you know for yourselves that, "These qualities are skillful; these qualities are blameless; these qualities are praised by the wise; these qualities, when adopted and carried out, lead to welfare and to happiness"—then you should enter and remain in them.' Thus was it said. And in reference to this was it said.

"Now, Kālāmas, one who is a disciple of the noble ones—thus devoid of greed, devoid of ill will, undeluded, alert, and resolute—keeps pervading the first direction [the east]—as well as the second direction, the third, and the fourth—with an awareness imbued with good will. Thus he keeps pervading above, below, and all around, everywhere and in every respect the all-encompassing cosmos with an awareness imbued with good will: abundant, expansive, immeasurable, free from hostility, free from ill will. [And the same for compassion, appreciative joy, and equanimity.]

(A 3:66)

It is interesting how the Buddha's teaching that is often quoted as a charter of how to make up one's mind is then taken a step further and used to lay out a strong foundation for practice.

This next sutta is a short one that might sound a bit obscure as I read it. Basically what it concerns is the result of *kamma*, based on scriptural teachings. One of the traditional ways of dealing with the fruits of bad *kamma*—dealing with some *kammic* obstacle or difficulty—is the commitment to skillful *kamma*, building up the bank account of good *kamma*. This is a sutta that gives a perspective on and certainly encourages this.

> "Bhikkhus, I do not say that there is a termination of volitional kamma that has been done and accumulated so long as one has not experienced [its results], and that may be in this very life, or in the [next] rebirth, or on some subsequent occasion. But I do not say that there is making an end of suffering so long as one has not experienced [the results of] volitional kamma that has been done and accumulated.
>
> "This noble disciple, bhikkhus, who is thus devoid of longing, devoid of ill will, unconfused, clearly comprehending, ever mindful, dwells pervading one quarter with a mind imbued with loving-kindness, likewise the second quarter, the third quarter, and the fourth quarter. Thus above, below, across, and everywhere, and to all as to himself, he dwells pervading the entire world with a mind imbued with loving-kindness, vast, exalted, measureless, without enmity, without ill will. He understands thus: 'Previously, my mind was limited and undeveloped, but now it is measureless, and well developed. No measurable kamma remains or persists there.'"
>
> (A 10:219)

What is being referred to is that no measurable *kamma* will come of this. None will persist. With the liberation of the mind with loving-kindness, the kammic potential of that attainment will take precedence over any other *kamma* and generate fortunate results and rebirth.

This is actually called "heavy *kamma*," but it's *kamma* that takes precedence over unskillful *kamma*. Taking the life of parents and killing an arahant: these are called "heavy *kamma*" on the unskillful side.

However, on the skillful side, heavy *kamma* is such as the attainment of jhāna, and the attainment of the liberation of the mind by the brahmavihāras. They take precedence. Stream-entry, paths and fruits, are heavy *kammas* because they take precedence over other forms of *kamma*.

> "What do you think, monks. If a man, from his boyhood onwards, were to develop the liberation of the mind by loving-kindness, would he then do an evil deed?"
> "He would not, Lord."
> "And not doing any evil deed, will suffering afflict him?"
> "It will not, Lord. How could suffering afflict one who does no evil deeds?"
> "Indeed, monks, the liberation of the mind by loving-kindness should be developed by a man or a woman. A man or a woman cannot take their body with them and depart; mortals have consciousness as the connecting link.
> "But the noble disciple knows: 'Whatever evil deeds I did before with this physical body, their results will be experienced here and they will follow me along.'
> "Loving-kindness, if developed in such a way, will lead to the state of non-returning, in the case of a monk who is established in the wisdom found here in this teaching, but who has not penetrated to a higher liberation."
>
> (A 10:219)

So there is the recognition of the strength of loving-kindness as the ability to undermine other tendencies within the kammic potential.

> "If, monks, liberation of the mind by loving-kindness is developed and cultivated, frequently practiced, made one's vehicle and foundation, firmly established, consolidated, and properly undertaken, eleven benefits may be expected. What eleven?
> (1) "One sleeps well; (2) one awakens happily; (3) one does not have bad dreams; (4) one is pleasing to human beings; (5) one is pleasing to spirits; (6) deities protect one; (7) fire, poison, and weapons do not injure one; (8) one's mind quickly becomes concentrated; (9) one's facial complexion is serene; (10) one dies

unconfused; and (11) if one does not penetrate further, one fares
on to the brahmā world."

(A 11:15)

Even if one does not realize some state of liberation, those are
all good things. I don't see anything that is a drawback here at all.

I'd like to plant some seeds to encourage you to go back to the
sources. The Buddha is the root. Sometimes the language is a bit
daunting and the repetition is boring, but there is this extraordinary treasure trove of teachings and liberating insight, and the
Buddha's tremendous ability to see things clearly. It is rare in the
world and certainly rare in the world of religious teachings. There
is a great blessing in being able to tap into the teachings that we
have inherited through our good fortune.

We can take this next period to sit, bringing those thoughts of
loving-kindness to mind, reminding ourselves of the various formulations—whatever resonates. One of the words used to describe
the brahmavihāras when one is accomplished in these meditations
is "immeasurable." The heart is not bound by constricted, contracted small-mindedness. One sets that aside and allows the heart
to shine forth in that which is beautiful.

In the teachings, there are what are called *vimokkhas*. One of the
vimokkhas (liberations or emancipations) is liberation through the
beautiful. This can be a meditative attainment in terms of color, the
kasiṇas, which are exceedingly beautiful. But it can also be a state
of mind like loving-kindness, which is a beautiful mind-state that
allows the mind to drop its self-concern, worries, fears, anxieties,
and comparisons and dwell in that which is truly beautiful. It is not
really about me being anything or getting anything. It's the beauty
of being able to put it all aside. Dwell in that wish of loving-kindness,
to be abundant, exalted, and immeasurable. We can take this time
to cultivate some of these qualities.

Questions and Answers

Question: In the palm-reader story, you mentioned that Ajahn Chah still had a lot of anger, but that he chose not to act from it. Does this mean that, for example, if there was a troublesome monk, Ajahn Chah would still experience a flare of anger but still have the wisdom to set it aside and consider what to do with a cool head? This sounds similar to what Ram Dass has said about his defilements: after so many years of practice, they are more like little neurotic shmoos that he can relate to in a relaxed way.

Answer: What the palm reader was looking at was fundamental temperament, karmic tendencies, the patterns that are there. Anger was a particular tendency that Ajahn Chah had, but through his ability to see clearly, he relinquished the tendency. The awareness had such clarity that the mind was not drawn to the tendency at all.

There was a very interesting circumstance that one of the Western monks had with Ajahn Chah. Ajahn Jayasāro, who is an English monk, was attending to Ajahn Chah and sitting with him, massaging his feet. A particular monk came in who had done something wrong, had been admonished for it and was undergoing a period of penance.

Ajahn Chah barked at him and scolded him, in what seemed to be a flare-up of anger. That was what was manifested. Ajahn Jayasāro, who was there massaging his feet, said that the peculiar thing was that there was absolutely no tension in his body. There was no manifesting of a mood or any kind of excitement. Ajahn Chah probably said to himself, "What this monk needs is to be ripped down one side and up another."

There was a similar circumstance that I had with Ajahn Mahā Boowa, who is well known for a couple of things. First, he is considered the arahant of the age in Thailand. He is in his mid-nineties now. He has been considered to be highly attained for a long time, and he is also well known for his ferocious tendencies.

I remember one time going to visit and spend some time with him. I had done a lot of practice at the time, and my mind was very still and clear. I was watching Ajahn Mahā Boowa speaking in a ferocious way, hearing the words and seeing his actions. But I was flooded with these feelings of joy and loving-kindness that I felt he was actually emanating.

You may be able to control anger, but it is different from when anger is not there at all. Certainly you were always quite careful around Ajahn Chah because you never knew which side was going to come out. It wasn't as if he was just playing with you, but it was as if he always responded to the situation or the person and there was no fixed way he was going to be boxed in: "Oh, I'm supposed to be a nice loving-kindness monk." You didn't want to get on the wrong side of him because he could be very direct and blunt.

Q: Would you explain the duties adult children have towards aging parents? And the duties of parents towards their children, as taught by the Buddha?

A: The Buddha taught that one should look after one's parents and try to care for their needs. In Asia, in general, that is very much a part of the cultural norm. One looks after one's parents. Of course, the parents have a duty toward their children of both helping and being role models for their children and grandchildren. In an ideal world, that is how it works.

The Buddha also said that the greatest gift that one could give to their parents, and I think it would work the same for parents towards children, is encouraging one's parents in virtue, generosity, and right view. There are material things that one can give to one's parents, and that is an excellent thing to be doing. However, it is even more beneficial and useful if one can encourage one's parents to establish themselves in a higher degree of virtue and generosity, as well as in aspects of right view and discernment.

Q: In a Dhamma talk several years ago, you mentioned an interview with a Christian monk. Reflecting on his forty years of monastic life, the monk said something about "I wish I'd been more kind." Reflecting on your thirty-five years in robes, do you have any lessons that stand out? I'm not interested in regrets, but the kind of wisdom-knowledge that the accumulation of years of practice illuminates.

A: It would depend on whatever is the thought of the moment as it comes out. It is also very encouraging that people actually remember Dhamma talks. I had forgotten I said that.

A strong lesson that pops out, picking at random out of the hat right now, is the aspect of patience. It is certainly something that Ajahn Chah emphasized over and over again. For myself that is one lesson that comes to mind: just be willing to be patient with things.

Sometimes we don't recognize the goodness that we are engaged in. Often our standards and expectations are high, and we judge ourselves in ways that reflect that expectation. We're not patient enough to recognize the goodness that we are actually doing. It's important to be present with that fundamental goodness that is a motivating factor in all of the things we do.

In respect to all of you who are on a retreat here, you wouldn't be here if you weren't committed to leading a wholesome, skillful life. And that commitment is often something not reflected on. Instead we think, "I've got to do this. I've got to do that. I've got to live up to this standard. This teacher said this. That teacher said that." It goes on and on.

So just be patient enough to set that all aside and say, "Well, what's really important to me?" Allow that to come into the heart and recognize it. And again, patience isn't just grimly enduring; rather, it is being able to be present with experience. That is how I relate to patience: that willingness and ability to be present with experience, so we can take it in and be present for it.

Q: Is it hopeless to send loving-kindness to Māra?

A: Well, Māra gets a bad rap. It depends on how we relate to it. Māra is the personification of the tempter. In the midst of being tempted with the desire of the moment, loving-kindness might not be the right tool. But in a bigger sense, that is the most important thing to have loving-kindness for, in the sense that loving-kindness is the wish for well-being. Māra is the epitome of the tempter, the personification of evil. That's a lot of suffering isn't it? The *kammic* accumulations don't bode well for him.

When we follow our desires and get caught in our views and opinions, how we suffer! That the whole construct keeps repeating itself: these are the forces of Māra. That's a worthy object of loving-kindness because there is so much suffering there. This helps turn our attention to the way out of suffering.

Q: When you have guided meditation in the past two afternoons, I've enjoyed slipping past the rapture and joy. I found the meditations incredibly grounding and at the same time streaming with energy. I'm finding it difficult to get past joy without your vocal guidance. Can you offer suggestions?

A: It's an experiential memory. It's good to remember that it's possible to go past that excitement of rapture and joy and be grounded in something that is very stilling, but still clear and spacious. So, tune in to the body because the body remembers these things. Come into the body, into the rhythm of the breath, the feelings and perceptions of joy, but allow oneself to move into steadiness and clarity.

Try to connect with it on a physical level, that is, with the tendency for energy, rapture, and joy. There can be a level of excitement that bubbles up. When we give an image to what joy does, it bubbles up. So move the energy down and through the body, allowing it to settle. That's a skillful way to work with it because once it comes up, it can feed into the proliferating mind.

Q: What are the characteristics of our personalities? Are personalities conditioned by *kamma* and our family, culture, and nationality? How do I learn not to take mine as true and real?

A: It's the suffering: that's how we learn to drop it and recognize the limitations, drawbacks, and pain involved. Certainly, personalities are conditioned by all that: past *kamma*, present *kamma*, family *kamma*, cultural *kamma*, nationality, gender, everything. It's all part of the conditioning process.

But then recognize its impermanence, instability, and changing nature. Because what we call our personality sometimes manifests like this, sometimes like that, depending on the people we are with and circumstance we are in. It isn't as if it's fixed and immutable. It picks and chooses. So learn how to recognize that, by seeing that changing, impermanent, uncertain nature. What we take as mine and me—it's not fixed at all.

Anicca is often translated as "impermanent or changing." Ajahn Chah would tend to translate the word *anicca* as "uncertain" or "not sure." I think that is an important shift. What is impermanent or changing tends to be objectified, whereas "uncertain" is much more subjectified: how I feel; how I experience things. It's an important shift. Bring it back into the subjective field of "how do I experience what I think of as moods, feelings, impressions, thoughts, or personality?" So one is seeing the suffering involved that inevitably comes up with those perceptions—the burden that I was talking about this morning, the limitation of being a dog tied to a post.

Also, it is important that we don't take it too seriously, that we are able to laugh at ourselves and the human condition, because taking it all very seriously weighs us down. In the end it is absurd. Life is sometimes "how did I walk into this Samuel Beckett play?"

Q: Just to clarify for my loving-kindness anxiety, are any phrases okay? And can they be said as a chant or at any speed? Is one more effective for attaining deep concentration?

A: The phrases have to have some sort of feeling meaningful to you. Is it meaningful to you? Does it resonate somehow? Because what is really important is not so much the phrases, but the feeling that arises, the feeling that is generated and established within the heart, loving-kindness.

As you cultivate meditation as a practice, it's helpful to have a few techniques, methods, phrases, and chants that feel comfortable to you because the nature of the mind is to get inured to whatever you are doing. No matter how good it is, you are going to get familiarized, and it is going to lose its potency, whether quickly or slowly. It's the nature of the mind.

Have a few tools. It's like when you have a tradesman show up at your house. You want an electrician to do something and he walks in with no tools or just one screwdriver. You are not going to feel confident that the job is going to get done. It's the same here. As we are practicing and cultivating, have some tools on your belt.

Q: Sometimes when I am concentrated, I have spontaneous body or facial movements. They may be large or just small twitches. Can you comment on this?

A: It's reasonably common. This is when an attunement with the body is quite helpful, and loving-kindness is very good with balancing that kind of energy within the body-mind complex, allowing that to unravel and untie. Whereas trying to concentrate too strongly or forcing the mind to have mindfulness tends to exacerbate things. So mindfulness practice that is broad and body-based lets that kind of energy flow through the body-mind. Then loving-kindness has a subsidiary effect of softening, replacing, and settling. These are good practices to work with.

Q: Is gladness the same as thankfulness?

A: In the chant in which the word is translated as gladness, the Pali word is *muditā*, which is appreciative joy, sympathetic joy, delighting in the goodness and success of others. So that's not quite the same as thankfulness. Another Pali word that is sometimes translated as gladness is *pāmojja*. That's a feeling of well-being, a kind of delight, a sense of feeling good about something.

Often the causal conditions in these sequences are a bit different: reflecting on virtue and the sense of non-remorse, a feeling of gladness arises. Reflecting on the truth of the teachings, gladness arises, or faith or confidence. Thankfulness is more gratitude, which in Pali is *kataññutā*. That feeling of thankfulness, appreciation, and gratitude has a different quality to it. So the word gladness is used in a couple of different ways.

Q: By the way, what does "Pasanno" mean?

A: It's primary meaning is one having faith, but also one having joy, sort of joyful faith.

Q: The near enemy of equanimity is aloofness. I've tasted both. One is much more familiar, and the difference is quite apparent. Can you provide any clues to identify subtle aloofness, which may not be so obvious, especially to the habituated mind?

A: One of the things that immediately comes up—I've mentioned it several times and then it also came up in the reading of the *Kālāma Sutta*—is how the Buddha asks if this is wholesome or unwholesome? Is it beneficial or not beneficial? So there is an immediate turning to what is kusala.

The near enemy of equanimity is aloofness or indifference. Indifference will always have a certain negativity, dullness, or slight aversion. It's sort of: "I don't want to deal with this, get out of my face."

Whereas equanimity, as a brahmavihāra, will be kusala: wholesome and associated with a sense of well-being, clarity, and presence. There is equanimity in the sense of being balanced, but it isn't a shutting out or holding at bay. There doesn't need to be. With equanimity we can be completely present with whatever is there because it isn't intimidating. It's not something that is fearful. It's not even strange. It's just the way it is.

We can hold something in a very wholesome space because it's not intimidating or fearful, and it doesn't stir up any aversion or negativity. It's just the way it is. So there is a clarity there. Tuning into kusala and akusala sorts things out very quickly.

Q: In your opinion, why do you think that Venerable Moggallāna is most often portrayed in suttas as a bit of an idiot and highly impractical while Venerable Sāriputta is portrayed as wise and skillful? Both were the Buddha's leading disciples. Is this possibly a result of translation or translators' view, or is this so in Pali also?

A: Actually, I think if anybody gets the short end of the stick, it is Ānanda, because he is a bit of a fall guy sometimes. But with all of his psychic powers, there is a certain spectacular quality to Moggallāna. He is also sometimes involved in sorting out certain problems within the Sangha. He is trusted, as well as proactive in dealing in Sangha matters.

I'm not so familiar with the Mahayana sutras. Certainly Sāriputta is often a fall guy in the Mahayana sutras. I'm not sure how Moggallāna comes across in the Mahayana sutras.

In regards to Anuruddha, there is a passing comment about when Ānanda had asked Anuruddha to sort something out and it didn't get done (A 4:243). The Buddha says, "Why did you even ask Anuruddha? You know what he's like. He's just not interested in practical matters." It wasn't a criticism. He was just the wrong person for the job.

I think one of the things is that in the Pali Canon, these great disciples come across as very human. They have personalities. They are distinct individuals.

There is a great sutta in which Sāriputta is sitting and meditating in the forest and Moggallāna, who is adept in psychic powers, sees this scene unfolding where there are two *yakkhas*, which is a type of celestial demon (Ud 4:4). They are flying along overhead and see Sāriputta meditating in the forest. It is the day before the Full Moon Day, and monks have nicely shaved heads.

One of the yakkhas says, "Look at that nicely shaved head. I'd just love to take my club and wallop it." And the other yakkha says, "I wouldn't do that if I were you. These sons of the Sakyan, they are pretty special sometimes. Be careful." The other says, "I don't know—that's a great target. I don't think I can resist." So he goes over, takes his club, and wallops Sāriputta over the head. The description is that he gives him a blow that could split a mountain.

Sāriputta is unmoved. Moggallāna has seen this scene unfold. Sāriputta comes out of his meditation, and Moggallāna asks, "How are you feeling today?" Sāriputta says, "Okay. But I've got a bit of a headache today." Moggallāna says, "It's no wonder, with these yakkhas." He relates the scene. "This is wonderful. These mighty yakkhas can give a blow to Sāriputta, and all he says is, 'I've got a bit of a headache.'"

Then Sāriputta says, "What's really amazing to me is that you can see these things happening. I didn't see so much as a mud sprite, let alone a yakkha, a deva, or anything like that." The sutta ends with these two great disciples admiring each other's qualities.

Q: What are the primary distinctions between Theravada, Mahayana, and Vajrayana?

A: Without confusing people, Theravada, just by the very literal translation of its name, means the teaching of the elders. Its primary focus is in trying to maintain the tradition as it was passed down as closely as they could assume were the original teachings of the Buddha. There are always some accretions and additions, but that has been its primary flavor.

It's also interesting that when the Dalai Lama gives teachings, one of the things he will do is invite Mahayana, Theravada, and Vajrayana monks to give blessings before the teachings begin. He will always invite the Theravadins to give a Pali chant because he will say that the oldest scriptures are in Pali, and these are the elder brothers within the Buddhist fold. He gives deference. It is very beautiful.

In Buddhist history, there was a range of schools. About 250 years after the Buddha, by the time of King Asoka, there were about eighteen distinct schools of Buddhism. Subsequent to that, there began to be a Mahayana movement, reinvigorating and redefining some of the principles. One of the main principles is putting emphasis on the Bodhisattva ideal.

The Vajrayana grew out of the Mahayana. There are several Vajrayana schools. Usually when someone says Vajrayana, they mean Tibetan. The Vajrayana schools in Tibet actually took many of the different schools and brought them to Tibet. One of the distinctive qualities of the Vajrayana is the emphasis on faith, ceremony, ritual, and the efficacy and use of that.

These are just snapshots. Of course, within these there are a huge number of schools as well. When you look at Buddhism, there is not a Theravāda tradition, a Mahayana tradition, and a Vajrayana tradition that are each homogenous and monolithic. A country like Thailand is considered very strictly Theravāda. But if you start looking and digging into the history of doctrinal and popular Buddhism, one thing looks like a Mahayana teaching and then another one looks like a tantric ritual. So there has been mixing and cross-pollination going on for millennia.

Q: What could American culture learn from Thai culture?

A: What immediately comes to mind is one of the first things you learn when you go to Thailand. There is a phrase, *mai pen rai*.

That would be a really good thing for American culture to learn. It means "never mind," as in, "Let go, it's not a big deal."

Mai pen rai: literally it means, "It is not anything." It allows people to navigate the thorny aspects of human relationships. *Mai pen rai.* That's the way it is. Never mind. There is no point in getting upset. *Mai pen rai.*

Of course, Thailand has been steeped in Buddhist culture for a long, long time. There is a book that was written by Phra Payutto; I don't think it has ever been translated into English. He had spent a few years in America as a visiting scholar at Harvard University and Swarthmore College and his English is very good. The book he wrote is about Thailand viewing America and America viewing Thailand—the interchange, the things each could learn, just seeing the possibilities.

That's one of the things for myself, having grown up in North American culture and having lived in Thailand for twenty-three years in a rural environment without speaking English and so being able to be steeped in a different culture. It was very helpful in being able to step back from my cultural conditioning. It isn't as if there is a perfect culture anywhere. The human condition is just not that way. You think, "Wow, if there was a culture that was steeped in Buddhism that would solve all the problems of the world." No, it wouldn't. There are human beings there. They'll create suffering wherever they go.

Closing Ceremony

*We can return to the things that we normally might
conceive of as ordinary and realize the power of
transformation that they hold: the power of the
refuges, the power of the precepts, and the power of
loving-kindness.*

First of all, I'd like to express my appreciation to Susan, Karen, and Cassidy for pulling this retreat together and being willing to step into the unknown: to see how to do it and take a chance on whether it actually worked or not. I've enjoyed my time here. I express my appreciation to all of you, the retreatants who came together and who have been interested and willing to pursue this exploration of loving-kindness. As I have tried to emphasize through this retreat, loving-kindness doesn't stand on its own. It is a part of a spectrum of the Buddha's teachings, both in terms of support of those teachings and also as a result of those teachings.

I would encourage you all to take what you have learned during this time back into the world—into the family, society, and workplace—and experiment on how to apply these teachings, how to sustain them. Having finished the retreat, whatever peacefulness, loving-kindness, and clarity you have cultivated, please take it with you. You don't need to leave it all here. Take it, share it, and recognize that it is a gift to other people as well. Sharing loving-kindness, virtue, and goodness: these are suitable things to share with others, and the world is desperately in need of them.

This simple ceremony that we have just done, the refuges and the five precepts, is something that is quite ubiquitous in Buddhist tradition. But I would encourage all of you to take it on board, investigate, and see how these refuges and precepts can both be an anchor for day-to-day life as well as the fruit of a skillful life well lived. Having a refuge, having an anchor in clarity of conduct, allows that virtue and holding to truth to be the basis of one's life.

I mentioned in one of the Dhamma talks that one of the most common formulations that the Buddha gives for the description of the stream-enterer, the first fruit of realization and liberation, was the stable confidence and faith in Buddha, Dhamma, and Sangha, and the stable commitment to the precepts. It is easy to overlook that as being ordinary. That's one of the problems we have as humans beings, we overlook the ordinary, being busy looking for something else. Of course, our whole life tends to be looking for something else to satisfy us, and we overlook the opportunities of satisfaction and contentment in the present moment.

We look for refuges, look for things to solve all our problems, for things to shore up our sense of well-being—just over there. And it is usually just out of reach as well. In contrast, we can return to the things that we normally might conceive of as ordinary and realize the power of transformation that they hold: the power of the refuges, the power of the precepts, and the power of loving-kindness.

On a certain level it is hackneyed and old: "May all beings be well and happy." You see it written everywhere in Buddhist texts, and you might even sign your emails with something like that. But recognize that there is a transformative power in it: an actual commitment and understanding of how to apply it, how to work with it, how to rely on it, and how to return to it allows it to be something that nourishes the heart and nurtures your day-to-day life.

The whole week that we've been here, what I've been teaching and emphasizing is pretty ordinary stuff. Certainly most people have heard it or read it at some time or another. But I think it's

when we make a commitment within ourselves to put it in to practice, give it the space to see if it works, and have the confidence to
stay with it for a while: that's when the transformation takes place.
It isn't as if somebody is going to get a new bit of information that is
going to transform them. It is rather the old and the ordinary that
is probably most useful.

Recognize, reflect, investigate, and allow those things to re-
verberate in consciousness. Be willing to keep experimenting,
applying, and seeing what are the new ways of holding a particular
perspective, practice, mode of conduct, or way of training oneself.

As for myself, this is my thirty-fifth year of being a monk, and
there are not a whole lot of new things that I learn. But what I *have*
learned is how to use the ordinary: the foundations that are so important, the things that are the ground of the teachings and our
training. As we develop a deepening appreciation and a deepening
skill in how to use these, then we see some radical letting go take
place, some radical willingness to put a lot of the things down that
we didn't want to be carrying around anyway.

So again, I would just like to express my appreciation to all of the
people who have helped out. Everybody helped out in this retreat in
the sense that, while you have been here, you pitched in; everybody
made it happen. That is worthy of appreciation. My own perception
of things, and what the organizers have told me, is that everything
has gone very smoothly. That is really appreciated when we come
together and practice: having a tangible example that when everybody pitches in, helps out, and harmonizes, then life goes pretty
smoothly. In the human realm, that's about as good as it gets.

Credits

The following translations have been reprinted with gratitude:

M 21, M 48, M 52, M 128: © 1995 Bhikkhu Bodhi. Reprinted from *The Middle Length Discourses of the Buddha*. Boston: Wisdom Publications.

A 1:575, 1:576–582, 1:583, 1:586–590, A 6:10, A 8:19, A 10:219, A 11:15: © 2012 Bhikkhu Bodhi. Reprinted from *The Numerical Discourses of the Buddha*. Boston: Wisdom Publications.

A 1:53: © 1999 Buddhist Publication Society. Reprinted from *Numerical Discourses of the Buddha*. Walnut Creek: AltaMira Press.

A 3:66: © 2003 Ṭhānissaro Bhikkhu. Reprinted from *Handful of Leaves*, Volume 3. Sati Center for Buddhist Studies and Metta Forest Monastery.

Many of the chants and reflections mentioned during the retreat can be found on Abhayagiri's website:

• http://www.abhayagiri.org/books/abhayagiri-chanting-book
• http://www.abhayagiri.org/audio

About the Author

Ajahn Pasanno took ordination in Thailand in 1974 with Venerable Phra Khru Ñāṇasirivatana as preceptor. During his first year as a monk he was taken by his teacher to meet Ajahn Chah, with whom he asked to be allowed to stay and train. One of the early residents of Wat Pah Nanachat, Ajahn Pasanno became its abbot in his ninth year. During his incumbency, Wat Pah Nanachat developed considerably, both in physical size and reputation. Spending twenty-four years living in Thailand, Ajahn Pasanno became a well-known and highly respected monk and Dhamma teacher. He moved to California on New Year's Eve of 1996 to share the abbotship of Abhayagiri Buddhist Monastery with Ajahn Amaro. In 2010 Ajahn Amaro accepted an invitation to serve as abbot of Amaravati Buddhist Monastery in England. Ajahn Pasanno is now the sole abbot of Abhayagiri.